W9-DEC-448

the Miraculous Escape

the Miraculous Escape

Jim Dimov

Fleming H. Revell Company
Old Tappan, New Jersey

Scripture quotations in this volume are from the King James Version of the Bible.

Library of Congress Cataloging in Publication Data

Dimov, Jim.
    The miraculous escape.

    1. Dimov, Jim.   I. Title.
BR1725.D55A33   266'.0092'4 [B]   74–22021
ISBN 0–8007–0694–3

Contents

Introduction

Is it true, or just a dream? Am I free, or am I under the influence of my imagination?

Dear Reader—you who are raised in the free world would never imagine how blessed you are! Many times while sleeping, I dream. I've seen myself back in Bulgaria, and I've asked myself in my dreams, "Why did I come back to my country? I know how bad it is, and still I am here in Bulgaria!" Once, as I was talking to one of my sisters, two militiamen arrested me. I turned to my sister and told her, "Tell my mother I'm going to see her real soon!" When I woke up, I realized I was in America. It had all been a horrible nightmare. With an unspeakable sense of joy and relief, I thanked God again and again for America.

Are you a person with a big heart? Of course you are! You should never underestimate yourself! In spite of the fact that God made the sun, which gives everybody life, you are greater than the sun, because the sun doesn't realize its existence. I am so happy to present this book to you, who are greater than the sun! I am so privileged to live in the greatest country in the world. That is what America is, through the eyes of a thankful foreigner.

It takes a lot of experience, a lot of ability, a lot of time, a lot of inspiration, and a real gift from God to write a successful book. This is my story—a living witness of the amazing way in which God has moved in my life, and He has not stopped moving.

Because I have not had a great deal of background in writing, I must draw upon the one true Source of inspiration, God Himself, to help me write a book that is not just another series of meaningless words. It must be a book that is useful, valuable, and above all, truthful. It is my fervent prayer that it will be a book which will make its way into your heart and give you a vivid impression of my life.

My decision to trust God completely for this project did not come immediately. In the beginning, I fell into the trap of trusting other people to take notes on my testimony and then to write a book in a professional way. One writer tried to steal my story by placing his name as the author and my name second as the subject of the book. Time after time my money was taken from me, but the book remained unwritten.

Finally, I decided to write the book myself, and here I am writing under the inspiration of the Holy Spirit of God, who is the only Safe Guide. And so, since deciding this, the thoughts before the lens in the camera of my memory have been quickened into focus and are rushing out from my heart to your heart. They are pouring out and forming into letters, words, and sentences, building a new book, bringing humor and pathos, laughter and tears.

May the Lord bless you abundantly and challenge your heart as you take a trip over the breathtaking road of the miraculous escape in my life.

the Miraculous Escape

1

The Colorful Events of My Childhood

I was born in a small village called Baraklii, which is close to Burgas, a city located on the shore of the Black Sea in eastern Bulgaria. My father was a clerk in the village hall and highly respected by every villager. He was tall, slender, and very ambitious. In spite of all his good qualities, he couldn't succeed in supplying all the needs of our family. Of course, as a child, I don't remember being hungry often, but I experienced much poverty. Still, I had a very happy childhood. Even though I was the baby of the family, I was never spoiled. On the contrary, I was always being called upon to help my older brother, sisters, and parents.

Our home was located close to a winding river where, as children, we had lots of fun. Often we went a long distance from the village, swimming in the muddy waters of the river, hunting frogs, roasting frogs' legs over an open fire, and eating them with big appetites. Frogs' legs are very delicious!

Winter time was entirely different. The river was extremely dangerous. Flooding was quite common. The swollen river would come like a blast, carrying wood, dead birds and animals, stones, and all kinds of junk with it. Often many houses were flooded and badly damaged. Some winters were very severe because of the snow, which was worse than the flooded river. A number of houses were completely covered with snow. Only the chimneys could be recognized by the smoke pouring out of them. For weeks, people were digging tunnels into the snow in order to get out of the houses. None of the homes had plumbing or sewers.

In our village, there were three sources of water. Natural water was permanently channeled through three-inch pipes without valves, running all year long and pouring out at last into a large, two-by-twelve-foot watering trough. Many sheep, cattle, horses, and other animals came to the trough to quench their thirst. Through an opening in one corner, the water spilled out onto the ground, making a lovely "swimming hole" for mosquitoes. During the summer, it constituted a serious loss of water. During the winter, the trough area was surrounded by ice and mud.

This was the only place where the people could get water for their needs. Spring, summer, and autumn, the village women supplied their families with water from there. They carried long, strong, handmade (frequently carved) poles called *cobilitsi* over their shoulders. At the end of the *cobilitsi* there were two slats where the handles of two buckets were supposed to hang without sliding.

Supplying water was the housewife's most difficult job. Very few women were able to get water in the winter time. (I would like the modern American lady to imagine herself in such a situation!) And so, the men were very important during the winter time. They not only took care of the water supply during those cold months, but they also took care of the wood supply all year round. Burning wood was the only way to cook a meal and heat the house.

Our home was not only the center of attraction for many of the villagers, but it was the only Protestant church in the village. My father was the preacher. He was not ordained by a denomination, but he *was* ordained by God. He was a very good speaker, and the Lord reached many souls through him for His glory. On Sundays especially, our home was packed with people, and many were saved. I have the sweetest memory of our home. Nothing on this earth can build a better citizen, a better personality, or a better character than the atmosphere of a spiritual, Christian home. It enables a person to build his life on a solid foundation, which gives the only true security through a simple faith in the Lord Jesus Christ.

My mother was Greek Orthodox when my father met her, and she deeply loved the Lord. In a very short time, she realized that in the Protestant faith there was more light. She soon accepted the Lord Jesus into her heart and became a born-again Christian.

It was 1942 when my father decided to go to the so-called New Lands, which had been given to Bulgaria by Germany. Many Bulgarians were attracted to the New Lands, which had once belonged to Greece.

One day after we had been there for a time, we heard that the New Lands were to be given back to Greece. All Bulgarians were to go back to Bulgaria. Some of the Bulgarians suffered grievously because they had been very mean to the Greeks. We heard how the beard of a Bulgarian Greek Orthodox priest had been pulled out, how the hands of children had been cut off, and many other atrocities.

Our neighbors and friends were begging us to stay there. They told us no harm would come to us. But my father was the one who made the final decision to go back to our country. We began to pack our luggage. We couldn't take many things with us because the vehicle could not hold very much. While we were carrying out our beautiful stove, it fell and broke into pieces. We tried to sell some of our belongings, but the sale was not very successful.

We arrived at the city of Burgas on the shore of the Black Sea and settled in my aunt's apartment, which was very old and in very bad condition. My aunt's family found better

accommodations, so we were very happy to occupy the one-
bedroom apartment. There were six members in our family.
Things were not very comfortable because there was not
enough room for such a large family. My father could not find
work so he finally had to take up his old job as a clerk in the
village hall. Having nothing to live on for a while was difficult, but we were happy to be alive and healthy.

Little by little, we adjusted ourselves to the new circumstances. The long winter went by and life became easier.
Springtime in Bulgaria is very beautiful. In that year, 1945,
I didn't enjoy the beauty of the spring because the weather
was so cold and we didn't have enough food and clothing. I
was eager to finish school and was looking forward to summer
vacation. I had some friends in school, but they didn't have
much to say to me because I was a Christian. At school, I
heard the teachers talking about the new system of rule.
They discussed nature and taught us atheism. I didn't like the
new poison of the old devil, but I had to go to school. At last,
school finished and the summer vacation began. I wanted so
much to have friends to play with but I was disappointed—
that's why I became a very lonesome Christian boy!

I had two uncles, Nick and George. My older uncle, Nick,
was a very rich man. One day, he invited us to live in his
house and take care of his property. There were two apartments in the house. My uncle's apartment had two bedrooms
and ours, just one. We did not know the convenience of an
indoor bathroom. My parents, my brother, and I slept in the
kitchen; my sisters, in the bedroom. The house was a very old
one, and we had to repair the roof often.

I loved to go to church, and while walking to the services
I prayed all the way; when I arrived at the church, oh, what
a difference! All the people who were dedicated believers
smiled and radiated the love of the Lord. Everybody was
reverent in the church. In the winter time, it was very pleasant to go to church.

Our Christmas was on the seventh of January. Usually at that time, we had a lot of snow. The church would be heated with four high wood stoves which made the church very warm and comfortable. Every Christmas we had a very beautiful play about the birth of Jesus. I used to take part in the children's program and one year I sang with some other boys, "We Three Kings of Orient Are." My solo was the verse, "Frankincense to offer have I; Incense owns a Deity nigh; Prayer and praising, all men raising; Worship Him, God on high." When the program was over, everybody received a sack of candies and nuts. The children especially, enjoyed that moment the best.

For three days, we celebrated Christmas. The choir was separated into two groups and visited almost all of the Christians who were part of the congregation. It was so beautiful when the group approached a home very quietly. Everyone walked softly on the fluffy snow, which made a crunching noise. The choir leader signaled and the group would begin to sing, "Silent Night," or other Christmas songs. Because it was late at night, the songs could be heard far away. Many neighbors would open their windows to hear the Christmas caroling better. Some of the people would tell us how much they enjoyed the singing.

"You are the last expression of the spiritual life of our country," they said. Later on, caroling in Bulgaria was forbidden.

We used to have very meaningful baptismal services on the Black Sea shore. Later on, these were forbidden also, and we had to baptize believers inside of the church in a pool constructed under the platform of the pulpit, to be used especially for this purpose. Baptism of children was forbidden in the church, and young people up to eighteen years old were not allowed to go to church at all. Of course, these things didn't happen all at once, but gradually, our freedoms in worship were banned.

I was saved and raised in a Christian home, but my faith was nurtured under the ministry of American missionaries. They were forced to leave my country in 1946. Many of the Christians went to say good-bye to them at the railroad station. At that time, a great desire came into my heart to become a missionary. However, because the situation in my country was becoming worse in every respect, my hopes seemed worthless. The mother of the missionary family, who was a widow, was the best Christian I have ever met. Her name was Olga. Her daughter, Mary, was my Sunday-school teacher. She also had another daughter, Martha, and a son, Joro. As we watched, Olga waved to us with a white handkerchief until the train disappeared.

The Russian army came to Bulgaria, under the pretext of liberating my people from the Germans, on the ninth of September, 1944. The Communists occupied Bulgaria and took control of all the ministries of the government. George Dimitrov became the president of Bulgaria. He was treated as a god in Bulgaria.

Later, he met with Tito to plan a way to join Bulgaria with Yugoslavia and make them one country. George Dimitrov and Tito were invited by Stalin to come to Russia, but Tito did not go. Dimitrov went feeling very happy and privileged to go, but he was brought back dead. In a short time, a great mausoleum was built in the center of the city of Sofia. Today, everybody can visit there and see the embalmed body of the first Communist president of Bulgaria.

It was Anton Yugov, the new minister of the Interior, who created the so-called People's Militia and People's Courts. A People's Coalition was also formed, including the Agrarian and Social Democrats.

The name of the city I lived in is Burgas. One hundred eighty thousand people live there. It is located in eastern Bulgaria on the Black Sea shore, and it is the main harbor of

Bulgaria. The main street, which leads to the seashore, is packed every evening with pedestrians. Sea gulls glide along the shore and all over the city.

Most of the people live in very small apartments. They use electricity instead of gas, and the people are required to turn it off after 10 P.M. Some of the bathrooms are outdoors. People are allowed government loans to build their own apartments, but they have to put in a great amount of money and wait sometimes ten or more years until their loan is approved. I know of some people who started to build their apartments without the necessary finances, and when the apartment was completed, their hair had turned white because of increasing government demands.

Usually, people use wood or coal stoves. There are no refrigerators. Very few people are privileged to have their food refrigerated. Almost all of the people have to buy their food daily, and that is very hard on them. Always there is a shortage of food in Bulgaria. Every family has somebody waiting in the food line at the store. Many times when their turn comes, the products they want are sold out.

Of course, the Communists go to special stores provided for them and get the best-quality food. They are very highly paid and they have automobiles and other vehicles, expensive apartments, and houses. They are very, very wealthy and we call them "red capitalists." As a glazier, I was sent to install a big sheet of glass in the new villa of a very rich Communist. He was expecting to get furniture, ordered from Paris, and that's why a special painter was decorating the walls to match the exclusive furniture. Especially the top Communists live like kings in every Communist country. The doors are opened widely when a person comes and shows his Communist identification.

When our missionaries went to America, they told the American Christians about the great financial need of the

Christian workers in our country. This moved the hearts of
the Americans and, in a very short time, they gathered a lot
of clothing and finances and sent them to Bulgaria.

I will never forget the great gift we received in 1947.
Raised in a very poor family, many times I used to go to
school absolutely hungry—not even a piece of bread for
breakfast. I would watch my school friends eating wafers and
sandwiches and my mouth would water as I looked at the
good things to eat. I never had long pants up to that time and
used to wear short pants with long stockings in the winter
time. When the clothing came from the United States of
America, everybody in my church was given clothing.

I remember two huge boxes arriving at my church in the
backyard. Two men opened the boxes, took the clothing to
the front of the church sanctuary, and spread out the things
to the right and to the left. All of the people were allowed
to help themselves and they matched the different pieces of
clothing as they chose. We received all kinds of clothing and
shoes. I was dressed like a millionaire's son! My heavenly
Father, who has unlimited riches, supplied my needs. More
than anything else, I was happy for a pair of pants. They were
blue with little, shiny, zigzag figures in the material. I was
overjoyed by the fact that I was wearing a pair of long pants
which fit me perfectly!

Many non-Christians were attracted because they wanted
to get some clothing, also. The evangelical pastors used to get
a little financial support before and after the Communists
took over Bulgaria. Because the value of the money of the
new system dropped so drastically, the pastors began to exchange their finances, not through the bank but through
some Jewish people who gave them much more than the
bank. After we received the clothing and the pastors received clothing and money, the Communists could not bear
that fact. Many times they had warned the evangelical lead-

ers in Bulgaria, "Your time will come!" At last, here was their long-awaited opportunity. All the pastors of the main evangelical groups were arrested and blamed for being Anglo-American spies.

All fifteen spiritual leaders were tortured until they lost their willpower and didn't realize what they were doing by confessing in public court that they were guilty of spying.

In spite of the circumstances, my desire to be a missionary was growing more and more. After the evangelical court trials, all the churches in Bulgaria were shaken. The condition of the churches compared with this Scripture:

> And the Lord said, Simon, Simon, behold, Satan hath desired to have you, that he may sift you as wheat: But I have prayed for thee, that thy faith fail not: and when thou art converted, strengthen thy brethren.

> Luke 22:31,32

Many of the Christians were frightened and later came to themselves like the Apostle Peter. Some of them denied their Christian faith and went into the world. Some of them became traitors. We began to serve the Lord even more strongly.

My desire to be a missionary continued to grow stronger every day. All kinds of plans for escape came to my mind. To escape by swimming was too far. In fact, I knew how to swim "like a fish." Sometimes I used to go so far out into the Black Sea, I could hardly see the people on the shore. A sudden fear would penetrate my being. I thought, "How deep the water is under me!" Then I would thank the Lord and begin to plead the blood of Jesus, and the fear immediately left me. Still, this way of escape was too difficult and not the Lord's way, anyhow. More and more the Communists secured the borders with modern radar equipment so escape became impossible in my thinking.

By this time, I had become a teen-ager and was thinking more maturely. I realized the necessity of learning the English language in order to go to the West. Over 50 percent of the newspapers are printed in English. All over the free world, English is accepted as the international language, but English was forbidden in Bulgaria. All the people who knew English and had lived in the West were careful about their position because they were under strong suspicion by the Communists.

My mother was taking good care of our family. My father was making a very low income as a clerk in the village hall, so we could hardly survive. Every summer, I had to work and save money to buy my school books and clothing. Of course, my father provided as much as possible, but still we were very poor. We "gave" all the property in the village as a gift to the government because we were forced to do so. I remember in the winter time, very often we ran out of wood and coal. All the windows were covered with unwanted but beautiful frost figures on the glass. Mainly, we tried to stick close to the wood stove, trying to keep warm by the fast-waning heat.

It was very inconvenient for us, being a six-member family, living in one bedroom and a kitchen. My sisters used to plug their ears with cotton in order to study their many subjects. My brother and I would read out loud. English was considered the language of the capitalists and was outlawed, so it was not taught in our school. However, I found some old English books and began to study very conscientiously, but I found English a very hard language to learn. Yet, I liked it so very much. Later, the Communists realized they were making a mistake about the English language. They finally came to the conclusion that in order to conquer their enemy, they should know the enemy's language! So English began to be one of the Western languages allowed in our schools. English courses began to flourish for adults. I began to study every day more and more words which I stored in my mind. It is strange how a person can dream of something which seems impossible. Physically, I was in Bulgaria, but mentally, I was already living in the West. It is amazing how a human being can live on his imagination. It is more amazing how the Lord makes that desire come true. So English was my best-loved subject of study.

Many times, the water pipes and the water meter cracked because of the water freezing in them. The ice expanded and did a lot of damage to the water system. We used to leave the faucet open in order to keep the water running and to prevent it from freezing. Very often, the city would cut off the water at the source in order to conserve it. All over the city, one could see hundreds of people walking on the street carrying big containers, searching mainly for drinking water. All kinds of troubles all winter long!

We spent many hours clearing away the snow in order to be able to walk out of the house. Often we melted the snow and used it to wash our laundry. All day long all of us were very busy—very active, sometimes happy, sometimes sad, and sometimes encouraged and inspired by the circumstances. We rejoiced in the Lord.

After spending all of our energy during the long winter day and ending up exhausted, we used to relax during our supper, later read the Bible, and after that, we went to bed. Our beds had heavy covers but still it was extremely cold. The sheets were icy cold, and I used to rub my feet one against the other for over an hour in order to warm them. Most of the winter we slept with heavy, handmade winter socks on our feet. My mother knitted during the summer and was successful in supplying all of us with winter necessities.

Many times, I used to heat a brick in the stove oven and wrap it with a rag and oh, what a joy! I had my portable heater in bed with me. It was enough to keep my feet warm all night long. Early in the morning, I heard the rough alarm bell of our clock. All the windows were frozen and everybody was breathing like steam engines. My nose and cheeks were blue and on the cover, I often found ice from my breath. The hot steam out of my mouth had turned to ice! I jumped quickly out of my bed and immediately began to rub my nose and cheeks. After that, some exercises caused my blood to circulate, and then I was ready for the fight with the merciless winter.

I would like to share with you, Dear Reader, something which was the main reason for our survival: We never stopped asking for guidance from the Lord, thanking and praising Him for His mercy and His love and for giving us the salvation prepared for us on the cross.

I recognized my Lord and Saviour to be the only answer to all of our problems, and the only way to get to heaven. How beautiful is the condition of a Christian who really loves the Lord! Every nonbeliever is miserable. I don't care how educated, wealthy, or in what circumstances you are, if you don't have the Lord Jesus in your heart, you are just miserable. Yet, you are not a hopeless case. There is hope for you right now. Just invite Him, the Lord Jesus, into your heart, and the joy of heavenly happiness will flood your being. Indescribable, glorious joy will flow through you, and you will taste a little bit of heaven while you are on the earth. I am absolutely convinced that without eternal life, this temporary life of ours has no meaning! Yes, Dear Reader, I was already a soldier in the army of the Lord.

So I continued praying, asking the Lord to help me to become a missionary. I kept growing physically, mentally, and spiritually; little by little, I began to improve my English and always, mentally, I was living in the West.

My father was very strict and wanted to give all of us an education. His favorite hobby was reading books.

My father used to share many stories with me, and I enjoyed listening to his educated language. He told me how a man used to go high on a mountain near a city where my dad studied in school, and there, played the flute. The echo of the flute could be heard very clearly in the city situated next to the mountains.

"By all means, you should study to play the flute," my father once said to me. He was the first one who told me how good life is in America and how democratic the American government is. All my dad told me and advised me to do turned out to mean a great deal to my future life. He told me never to get involved with alcohol, cigarette smoking, and immoral life. Nothing is more precious than Christian parents! How valuable was his advice and training!

One day, my father couldn't go to work because he felt very sick. A little later, he was sent to the hospital where the doctors discovered widespread cancer in the abdomen. At that time, there was an awful flu epidemic all over the city. The flu got hold of my dad and in a very short time, he became skin and bones.

I was sad because I was not going to have a dad very long. I dearly loved him. I took care of him, helping him by moving him from one room to another because he thought he would feel better if he changed places. Many times a day, my father called me to give him a drink, food, or to help him to move into another room. I always responded immediately, and being very strong for my age (I was seventeen), I used to pull my dad's body up from the bed, grasp him around the waist, put his arms around my neck, and help him to walk through the little hallway into the bedroom. In an hour or so, again I was happy to please my dad by helping him to move into the kitchen, which was used as another bedroom. My father never lost his faith in God in his heart, and there was always a smile on his face.

It was late afternoon and I was splitting wood in the basement. I was praying to the Lord to help my dad when I heard my mother's voice calling me into our kitchen. I went immediately.

"My son, your dad is going to be with the Lord real soon. Go to him and ask him to forgive you," she said.

We have a custom in Bulgaria: when a person is passing through the door of death, his loved ones are to ask the "traveler" to forgive them if they have done something wrong to him.

I approached my dad's bed very quietly, looked at his pale face, and smiled to comfort him. It took a lot of willpower to control my emotions. He smiled at me and asked me through his eyes why I had come to him.

"Dad, please forgive me if I've done something wrong to you."

"May the Lord forgive you, son, and I forgive you, also. Be obedient to the Lord and to your mother. May the Lord bless you and prosper you abundantly."

I wanted to cry, but I couldn't. My throat was choked and my tears were blocked. I was on my knees praying for my father and watching his every movement. He asked me to give him some water. I got a glass of water, lifted his head, and helped him to drink. He couldn't swallow much water and laid his head back on the pillow. Then he smiled at me and thanked me for helping him. I was observing every move of my dad's eyes and lips, and was trying to enjoy every second of my father's life. I realized that on this earth, I would never have a dad to advise me and help me in my youth again. In a few more moments, I would have to depend completely on my heavenly Father.

My dad was smiling, and I could see the corner of his

mouth was moving slightly. Probably he was seeing the glory of the Lord. He began to breathe more and more slowly. Finally, he took a very deep breath and won the battle! I was holding his hand, which was very cool. Then my dad blew the air out of his lungs for the last time and gave up his spirit to the Lord. The quietness of his death filled our kitchen. My dad had gone to be with the Lord.

Yes, my dad had won the victory in battle! Before it was dark, about 5:00 P.M., he won the competition and left us, at fifty-two years of age, on the twenty-ninth of April, 1952. I was seventeen years old and had to face the raw reality and fight for my future life alone, without a father.

2

From Worker to Soldier

Not very long after my father died, my older sister got married and my brother was drafted into the army. After two years in high school, I transferred to a technical trade school called "George Dimitrov," the name of the first Communist president of Bulgaria. My main subject in school was mineral flotation, a process by which, through machines, water, and chemicals, the stone is separated from its useful components. I had to study seventeen subjects, and for some of the most difficult ones, there was no printed matter.

Being without a father, I was allowed nine dollars a month support from the government. With the money, I could get some supplies for school and buy a little food. I got permission from the director of the school to go to work at the harbor of my city of Burgas. I worked eight hours a night and attended school during the day. It was extremely difficult to work, go to school, and prepare for seventeen subjects. Many times I went to school absolutely hungry, without even a piece of bread for breakfast. I often fell asleep on the classroom bench. I was not able to bear the load of so many undertakings. Later on, I stopped working and concentrated on studying my subjects.

After three years I finished the trade technical school, and immediately began to work as the most common worker at the biggest chemical-flotation factory, about fifteen miles away from my city. I had to work four shifts in a month. Every week was a different time and the worst of it all was

I had to work on Sunday. It was so painful to my heart not to be able to go to church.

I had a number of bosses and none of them had any education. They knew how to write a little but were very poor in reading. Once in a while, they asked me to read an article from the newspaper to the crew because they couldn't read fluently. All of them were afraid of losing their jobs because of trained technicians like me, and yet all of them were members of the Communist party of Bulgaria, which was their strength. They treated me very badly in order to discourage me and to make me quit my job. I was given the worst jobs all the time.

I tried to witness for Christ to some of the boys and the news was carried all over the factory. There was a boy, John by name, who was totally atheistic. He was not educated at all and had a very hard time expressing himself in proper Bulgarian. Very often, he came up to me with his hands in a praying position in order to mock me. I smiled at him and was very sorry for the poor atheist. It was good news for my bosses to find out I was a Christian. People who believe in God are not supposed to be leaders in any company in Bulgaria. When I had enough experience as an apprentice in every department of the factory, I realized the director of the factory wouldn't advance me according to my education because I was a Christian, so I wrote a letter to the government of Bulgaria. A letter was sent to me in response saying that I would be hired immediately as soon as there was an opening.

I worked one year and eight months under the same conditions. Many times, I went to sleep on my feet. Often, I almost fell into the flotation machine. I had to travel by bus two hours, before and after work. Altogether, it took me twelve hours a day, six days a week. Very often we had workers' meetings where a Party leader would say, "Every piece of copper must be used as power in the bullet against the enemy," and he meant America. All this hardship was beneficial to me because I discovered a strong willpower in myself.

While my brother was in the army, I tried to delay my army service as head of our home. After close to two years of torturous work, I was drafted because my brother had completed his obligation to the army and now could help with the family.

I went to serve my military duty in the same city of Burgas, and because of my technical chemical education I qualified, not by test or choice, but by an order, to be in the chemical army division. I felt very miserable when I found myself without hair (we had to cut our hair very short soon after being drafted), and among all kinds of characters. Most of the boys were not educated enough to be chemists, but were forced to study during their service.

In my room in the barracks, there were about 140 people. The sergeant insisted on the windows being closed all night long. Because of the dirty rags which were used instead of socks, the air was unusually heavy with smelly odors. We were allowed to go to a common bath in the city once a week —sometimes, once in three weeks. Almost everything was detrimental to the health of the soldiers, but some of the exercises turned out to be very useful. The weaker soldiers got sick and were sent to the hospital.

Our division of thirty or forty men was camping in a forest where we experienced the most severe weather. One day our captain was inspecting the guns of the men involved in chemical warfare. He discovered two or three very tiny dots of rust on the guns which belonged to me and to a friend of mine. Right away, we were commanded to put on our dress uniforms, get our guns, and fill our soldiers' sacks with bricks. Then we were ordered to run and lie down at once. The heavy load was many times heavier while we were lying down. This punishment continued for more than one hour. A shepherd was close by when we were lying on the grass, and he said, "Throughout the entire Turkish slavery of Bulgaria, never was such torture known."

Words cannot describe the pain caused by the load of bricks on our backs while we were lying down! After such harsh treatment, we couldn't come to ourselves for a long time.

It was a very rigorous winter. During my guard-duty hours, I had to jump up and down in the snow around a bush in order not to freeze. Every soldier had to dig a trench about a foot deep in the ground for his own tent. Most of the tents were flooded after the sun began to melt the snow. We had to dig a deep hole in the ground inside the tent in order to channel the cold water away from our sleeping quarters. In a very short time, the holes were filled and all of us used our only food containers to take the "mean" water out of the tent.

With all these extreme circumstances, we were learning how to defend our country, how to protect ourselves, and how to kill people with guns, missiles, and bombs, which I heartily disliked. However, we were forced to learn that devilish way of destroying people. How could I, being a Christian, hate to a point of killing others in order to live? They, however, repeated to us often that if we didn't kill, the enemy would kill us.

Then spring came and the conditions improved. Still there was ice and the water was very cold. While marching for training, we were crossing a small but very muddy stream. At once, we heard a sharp command from our lieutenant to lie down! Nobody obeyed. He got very mad and threatened all of us with severe punishment. So we had to lie down in the ice water, holding our guns up in the air. The gun was much more valuable to him than a human being. There was a song which the soldiers sang: "O my dear carabino [gun], for us, it is our duty and honor to our dear country to serve it faithfully today."

The gun was treated like a living being. If anybody lost his gun, soldier or officer, he was arrested immediately and sent to prison for five years.

One day, a lieutenant came and chose all the boys with high-school and technical-trade training to go to a town called Itos to become part of an artillery division. I was trained to be a tank gunner on a big tank made in Russia. All the guns and ammunition were made in Russia, also. Above the gun of the tank was written in the Russian language, *Pomnie vrag podslushvaet,* which means, "Remember, the enemy is eavesdropping." This time, I was trained to destroy tanks. From chemical warfare, they made me a tankist.

It was a hard life in the army. The only pleasant time I had was when I was able to go to church or play my flute. I rented a very old flute before I was drafted, and I enjoyed practicing.

One of the officers, Captain Videlov, who had taken notice of my neatness, nice attitude, and my ability to accomplish things quickly, chose me as his special personal contact, just for cases of emergency. My commander was Sergeant Brastinkov. He was very tall, dark, and had a mean, long face. Any free time he had was used to choke himself with cigarette smoking. He was a person who couldn't breathe without smoking like a chimney. He was raised in a village and had a great contempt for city boys. In the very beginning, he warned me that he was going to fix those boys from the city. He sent the city boys to the most difficult places to work and gave them the hardest physical exercises.

One day in conversation, the Communists discovered that I was a Christian. The whole artillery division was shaken up. In fact, I never did hide my Christian faith. I was just waiting for the right time and the right person. All the soldiers and officers were surprised to find out that Jim Dimov was a Christian. Some of the men began to make fun of me, but some respected me more than ever before.

All the leaders of the division under the supervision of Major Madin, the political-party chief, were called together for a meeting in one, big room in order to question me, to put me in a position to prove me wrong. The Spirit of the Lord gave me the answer to all of the questions just as the Scripture had said (Luke 12:11, 12). When they asked me a question, immediately a spiritual and deep answer came forth. When I asked them a question, they couldn't answer it. All of them were very miserable because they were sincerely convinced of the foundationless poison of atheism. All of them literally gave up and were confounded. Major Madin told me, "You may believe, but I forbid you to talk to others. If you dare to talk about God, I will send you to jail."

My situation was very grave. To go to jail as a Christian did not frighten me. I was not afraid of that, but he could bring other political charges, and my future could be destroyed. I would be punished if I didn't obey him, and the five years in prison were guaranteed.

"Because you have commanded me, I will not tell about my faith in Christ," I told him, "but I will explain to anybody who comes to me why I believe in God and why I am a Christian. I would never neglect the opportunity to witness for Christ!"

After that, nobody came to me to talk about God! Before I talked to the political Communist party chief, many boys, sergeants, and officers discussed the subject with me. I felt that many would be saved if there were freedom to preach to these hungry souls.

My captain, Videlov, was shocked more than anybody else —his personal contact, a Christian! Immediately, a meeting was scheduled and now was the time for Sergeant Brastinkov to pour out his venom. He got up first and began to say things I would never have thought about saying. He was blaming me for my faith, for not obeying him, and he developed all kinds of foolish accusations. I noticed that his face was turning green. He was very nervous and couldn't breathe for a long time if he didn't have a cigarette to smoke. I was waiting patiently to hear the other accusations and charges which were formed in order to ruin my reputation.

Captain Videlov then got up and made the most devil-pleasing statement of all. He said, "Our Communist party is preparing faithful followers out of the Dimitrov youth organization. The youth are in a big container, like pieces of pumpkin boiled together in sugarcane syrup, in which the Communist party has its hand and chooses wonderful, free-thinking [a person who does not believe in God] boys for the greatest commission in the world—to destroy capitalism and to establish communism all over the world, which is the dream of all mankind, and right here in the midst of us, we didn't know we had a wolf among the sheep."

He discharged me publicly from assisting him because he couldn't trust me anymore. I was listening to him and was wondering at how devilish an atheist could be. I was also very happy because it is written:

> Blessed are ye, when men shall hate you, and when they shall separate you from their company, and shall reproach you, and cast out your name as evil, for the Son of man's sake.
>
> Luke 6:22

I was given an opportunity to say something, and again the Lord put words in my mind. Very gently, I explained my

spiritual condition and without hurting anybody, proved to
all of them that the accusations were just false charges and
didn't have any foundation, but that my faith in the Lord
Jesus was the reason for the attacks against me.

For about three months, I was not given permission to get
my city weekend pass. One dark night after dinner, I crawled
through the fence and began to sneak slowly away until I was
out of sight. In a very short time I was in church, where we
sang songs, prayed, and praised the Lord. I asked the Christians to pray for me, and they laid hands on me and prayed.
I felt the power of God all through me and felt stronger than
ever before. Nobody discovered my absence, which was a
miracle!

One day I received a letter from my mother, who promised to visit me on Sunday. I was very happy when my
mother and a neighbor lady came to see me.

"Your cousin from England is here," said my mother, "and
she brought you a beautiful silver flute from England." I
began to jump with joy and was trying to figure out a way to
go to see my cousin and her family. I thanked my mother and
our neighbor for the visit and for the news. They returned
home by train from the village. That same day, I approached
one of the officers, Lieutenant Uzunov, and told him the
news. He realized how much I would enjoy seeing my cousin's family and receiving the brand-new silver flute.

He told me, "Go, and remember, I don't know anything
about your absence."

I thanked him profusely and when the right time came, I
left. On the way, I tried to visit a schoolmate of my brother
in the same village, but he was not there. I explained the
circumstances to his mother and asked to borrow some of her
son's clothing. I was given a pair of pants, a sweater, and a
school hat; I thanked the lady and left. It was a long distance
to walk, and I felt very tired. All the time I kept praising the

Lord and asking Him to protect me and to give me strength for the long trip. The Lord answered my prayer very soon, and in a very unusual way. I saw a water-buffalo keeper coming toward me.

"I presume you are a soldier, aren't you?" he questioned.

"Yes, and I am very anxious to go home," I replied.

"Don't worry; I will help you," said the man.

I noticed a car in the distance, coming toward us. The man went to his buffaloes and drove them to the highway, where he blocked the road. The driver saw the cattle and stopped.

"I am sorry," said the kind buffalo keeper. "I purposely stopped you with the cattle. Would you like to help this soldier by driving him to the city?"

"Of course, I will be more than happy," the motorist answered agreeably.

I was amazed at the cleverness of this village man.

"Thank you so much," I said. "May God bless you!"

"That's all right," answered the good man. "Good luck to you." I thanked the Lord for helping me to get home.

My mother was very happy to see me again. It was a joy to arrive in such circumstances, safe and sound. I had a suit which was not made well, and I didn't like it at all, but having no choice and no time to wonder about it, I put on my suit and shoes. My heart was beating very fast. To get to see my cousin's family and to get a new flute at the same time—this was indescribable joy—and to be related to somebody from the West!

I went to my cousin's home. She lived with her parents in a very small house. All over the bedroom, I saw all kinds of presents brought from England. Nothing interested me but the flute. My cousin smiled at me very warmly and gave me the flute. I took it with trembling hands and could hardly believe it was true. The flute was in a square, white box. I opened the box and saw the three parts laid on red velvet.

It had wonderful tone. Of course, after I found that she expected it, I paid the full price for it in payments.

Again with very careful traveling, I rejoined my army division and nobody noticed my absence. For an unlawful departure in the army, a soldier could spend five years or more in prison. But God had His mighty hand on me.

One after another, the days flew by and the time for ending my service in the army was drawing closer and closer. Every day I was waiting, waving to the civilians, and praying to the Lord to help me get out of that army hell so I could prepare for my missionary work ahead of me. A date was set for our discharge, but our time of service was extended. It looked like the Lord was teaching me to have patience. At last, the time for departure came. I had been drafted as a chemist, later was made a tank gunner, and finished as a lowly soldier. But who cared! Now I was out of the army and was able to rejoin my church and serve the Lord with great happiness.

3

As a Civilian—
Out of the Army

I approached a "man of the world" who was working as a glazier. The man hired me to help him, but only on the condition that there was enough work. I accepted the offer immediately.

My new boss was heavyset, of average height, and very slow. I was supposed to carry sheets of glass by hand, to take off all wooden frames in the building, and bring them into a room where my boss was supposed to cut and install the glass in the frames. After the job was finished, I was to hang all the glazed frames back in the right place.

Being extremely quick, I succeeded in supplying all the materials, even to the mixing of the putty with varnishing oil to make it easy to use. When everything was finished, I tried to help my boss by cutting glass, but he didn't like the idea. I couldn't figure out why he pulled the sheet of glass out of my hands. My impression was that he didn't want me to learn how to cut glass, and I was right.

He had worked for years as a glazier and yet was not a good glass cutter. His hand was not steady during the cutting of the glass, which didn't make a straight, smooth moving of the diamond over the glass. Many sheets of glass were broken, but he didn't care.

I saved some money and bought my own glass cutter. During our lunch hour, my boss used to ride his bicycle home.

One day, I brought my lunch with me and in a few minutes, I finished eating and went and began to cut pieces of glass. The same day, I worked out a routine for operating the diamond glass cutter. When my boss returned, he was surprised to see how many frames were glazed.

"Oh, maestro!" he chided.

I sensed he was not pleased with my action. A few days later, he fired me. However, it was for my good! I approached a builder and asked him if he would allow me to install the glass in the building that he was responsible for. He gave me the opportunity and for the first time, I started to install the glass all alone.

In the Cooperative Home Builders' administrative building I made enough money to buy a bicycle, and I was very happy to have this vehicle. Now I could carry my tools and once in a while, I could carry a few sheets of glass, holding them against my body with one hand. Once, my former glazier boss saw me carrying glass on the street by hand and walking toward a building.

"You are crazy to carry glass by hand," he said.

I didn't say anything to him. I wanted to get a few sheets of glass from a glass company because I had found a private job. I went ahead and finished the job and got my money. I continued working there and saved enough to buy the material for a new suit. After I got the cloth a friend of mine and I went to one of the best private tailors in town, who promised to do a very good job. He showed me the men's catalog and my attention was drawn to an Italian-style suit. A few weeks later, he had the suit ready and oh, I cannot describe the joy of having my own first suit made out of the best fabric, called *lasticutin*.

Once a Christian boy named John came to our church. He was very handsome and had a winsome smile, but he was very naive. One day, he came to me and said, "Jim, I would like to talk to you."

He asked me if I would hire him to work with me. In spite of the fact that I did not have enough work for myself, I told him, "John, come and join me. When we have enough work, both of us will be happy; if not, we will struggle together." So he came to work with me as my helper. John was not very skillful, but he was very conscientious and sincere. However, later on, he began to stand on his own two feet financially because the Lord blessed him through the new trade

I finally succeeded in paying in full for my flute and was so happy to be able to go to church with my new suit, new shoes, and new flute. The Christians in the church were very happy for my success, but my mother was especially proud of me. Quite a few mothers who had unmarried daughters became very friendly with my mom. Some of them began to visit our home, which continued to be a meeting place for prayer.

I asked the Lord to find the right girl for me who would share the supreme desire of my dream to become a missionary. According to an old custom in Bulgaria, the parents arranged the marriages of their children. I had always thought this was wrong, and I was glad that my mother had the same understanding. Yet, I did not want to follow any man-made custom, but only to obey the Word of God regarding my marriage and missionary dream.

The time went by and I continued to study English, to work very hard, and to pray to the Lord to help me see my dream come true. One day after another went by and my desire to become a missionary grew so strong and so big, I felt within myself not only a burning desire but a vision of reality —a real fire which occupied all of my heart, mind, and being. Talking to the Lord, sincerely praising Him, and singing and praying kept me in constant communication with Him.

In the meantime, the persecution of the church and individual Christians continued. The Communists never failed to disturb the believers. Once they arrested a Christian friend of mine. Two Communists beat him badly because he was preaching the Gospel and didn't obey them when they forbade him. This young man was a former neighbor of mine, and I had invited him many times to church. During the partisan (guerrilla) movement, he helped those people, and that placed him in a favored position by the Communists; but once I invited him to come to church and he did come, with the purpose of criticizing our Christian faith. He said, "I am going to visit your church, but I will show you how foolish you are to believe in God in this twentieth century. Today, people are too well educated to believe in supernatural power."

I told him, "That's perfectly all right. You come anyway."

That very night after the sermon, he raised his hand and they allowed him to express himself. My heart almost stopped when, instead of spouting accusations, he raised his hand dramatically and said, "Tonight, I accept the Lord as my personal Saviour!"

Another friend of mine was arrested and also beaten badly. One of the Communists told him if he continued to preach, he would kill him.

"I am willing to die anytime," answered my friend. "But remember, after you kill me, ten Christians like me are going to be raised up by the Lord, for His Gospel is going to be preached! Remember, also, you are going to give account to God, and there is someone who is going to require explanations for your action right here in this city." By this, he meant his own father, who was a Communist.

The devil was trying to destroy the church, but the Lord was refreshing our hearts with His abundant spiritual blessings. The Communists broke the glass of the church again and again, which kept me quite busy replacing it. Some backsliders came to church. Some of them were traitors; some of them repented before the Lord.

One day, our pastor was ordered to leave the church for teaching young people how to defend Christianity. The youth meetings were forbidden. Children and young people up to eighteen years old were not allowed to go to church. Once, two deacons pushed a mother with a little baby out of the church. They told her, "You are not allowed to bring children to church."

The Communists persecuted the church more and more. Still, the Lord added new souls to the church, and we were very encouraged.

Every summer on a special day, we used to go outside the city to have water baptisms. It was so beautiful to watch this event. One summer day that year, I got up early, about 4:30 A.M., full of joy, and started to walk to the place of the baptismal service on the Black Sea shore. It was a very beautiful morning. Just when I arrived at the right place, the sun rose. It looked like it was coming up out of the waters of the Black Sea! I was fascinated by that view. My heart was thumping in my chest and I was joyfully looking forward to seeing the new people rejoice as they went under the water, burying the old person, and coming up from the water, a new creature in the Lord. However, to my great surprise, nobody came. I had been forced to work on Sundays by the Communists and in my absence, it had been declared that public baptisms were no longer allowed. So I went home broken-hearted.

I continued to pray more urgently and to work harder than ever before. But the company ran out of glass and in three months, I worked only four days. Once, I saw a friend of mine making molding and ornaments out of plaster in an apartment. I watched him about half an hour and memorized the details of the work. Then I went to a village, riding on my brother's little motorcycle. In that village, I was supposed to see a plastering expert. I introduced myself to him and asked him if he would draw on paper a few models of the molds for making ornaments and moldings. He took a piece of paper off a sack of cement and immediately drew a few pictures. I thanked him very kindly and went home. In the most primitive way, with a chisel, hammer, and a couple of files, I made forms for different profiles and was ready to go to work. At that time, some glass came and I was able to work again. My friend, John, was also very happy.

Every Thursday, we had a testimony service in the church. It was actually the best service of our church. Many Christians had an opportunity to praise the Lord for His love and for miracles in their lives. I praised the Lord also and told my brethren how much He had blessed me spiritually and financially. After the service, a young man by the name of Pavel came to me and asked me if I would allow him to work with me as a glazier. He described the struggles of his family— they didn't have enough food to eat and he needed to work very badly.

I told him, "I would love to help you if you will have a little patience. I cannot promise too much, but the Lord is preparing something else, so pray to the Lord to make the new business work out."

About a week later, John and I were installing glass in a very big apartment building. All the apartments were private. People borrowed money from the government with a little down payment, and had to repay it for sometimes thirty years. The owner of one of the apartments came and introduced himself to me. He saw that I was the glazier of the building. He was a very nice-looking Armenian. Later on, I found out he was a hairdresser and had his own shop. At that time, small, private shops and businesses were still allowed.

I told the Armenian, "I heard you are going to make plaster ceilings with ornaments. I can do an excellent job for you. I will make you happier than anybody else! Would you like me to do the work for you?"

"No," said the Armenian, like a very proud owner of much

property. "I have somebody already. His name is Cherven-kov, and he is an expert."

The next day, the proud Armenian came to me smiling and not so proud as the day before. He asked me, "Do you know something?"

"No, I don't," I replied.

"I like you very much. Here is the key to the apartment, and you may start to work anytime."

I was very happy to have the offer, and told him, "Thank you for trusting me. You will never be sorry for giving me the job, I assure you."

After the Sunday-evening service, I told the young boy, Pavel, to come to work. Pavel was very happy. John was not so happy. He wanted to be with me alone in order to have enough work. I told him, "Brother John, I understand your position, but remember, Pavel is our brother, and the Lord wants us to help each other. Pavel's family has been strug-gling for a long time."

"Didn't we decide to work—just the two of us?" asked John.

"You are right, but the Lord wants us to help Pavel. Shouldn't we obey the Lord first and change our decision?"

John gave up and we became three. We got the plaster into the living room, installed a special table made out of thick board and sawhorses for the work, locked the door behind us, and began to work. John and Pavel didn't know the slightest thing about this type of work. I knew how to do it, but I had never done it before. This was the kind of assurance the Lord put in my heart. Then I asked my friends to pray with me.

I said, "Lord, take our hearts, hands, minds, and beings and use them for Your glory."

It is very important in everything to have faith in God. At the end of the prayer, I said, "Lord, I thank You in advance for helping us."

I mixed the plaster with water, poured it on the table, and pulled the form over the soft plaster. From one side of the form, there was a leader board to control making the molding straight. In a few minutes, I realized I was not as fast as I should be, so I wasted some plaster. The second time, it worked much better. In about half an hour, I was experienced in forming the molding. The form turned out very nice, so we had a beautiful molding in front of us. The next step was to install the molding on the wall in the corner between the wall and the ceiling.

"Praise the Lord," I said. "It looks beautiful!"

About one hour later, somebody knocked on the door. "Who is it?" I asked.

"Jekky, the owner," said the proud Armenian.

I ran to the door and opened it. "Come on in," I invited him.

He looked up at the new molding, which was very different from the molding in the other apartments.

"It looks beautiful," said Jekky. "Lock the door; don't let anybody come in; and continue to work."

When I finished the molding, I said to Jekky, "I have a great idea about your ceiling."

"Go ahead and do what you have in mind, and I will pay any amount you want," he said.

So I did a much smaller molding around the ceiling and spaced this second, smaller molding a foot away from the other one. At equal distances I installed short, tiny, straight pieces of forms on the design of the plaster, and it became an unusually attractive ornament. It took one week to complete the job, and when Jekky inspected the work, he was delighted. In the evening of the last day on the job, I went to his home and told him the price. His ears began to turn red. I comforted him by explaining that somebody else would have charged him much more. And besides, he had said, "any amount." After recovering his composure, Jekky said, "Here is your money," and he began to count out a large amount of cash. By this time, his ears were completely red, but his face was happy.

When his neighbors saw the job, they asked me to do their work also. Jekky told me he would poison me if I did something better for them than I had done for him. A month later, Jekky found out he was the first man I ever did plaster ornaments for, and he said, "Did you really use my apartment as a testing field?"

John answered instead of me, "Are you happy about it?"

"Very much so!" Jekky exclaimed.

"Then don't worry about being the first one!"

Plaster ornaments were very popular at that time. Quite a few customers made contracts with me, and I made a lot of money.

Then Pavel asked me if he could get $2.50 a day. I told him it would depend on how much the Lord was going to bless us. An average worker in Bulgaria was getting approximately $1.00 a day. By working six days a week, a laborer was able to buy two pairs of shoes. So Pavel wanted more than twice the regular wages. All day long, Pavel sat on a chair at a table, putting the finishing touches to the forms which were to be installed between the two moldings. I myself did the heaviest work. All day long, I had to work on a ladder bent over backward, facing the ceiling, which is a very hard job. However, the customer whom we were working for liked the work so much!

He told me, "Jim, I don't have the money now, but if you trust me and will do all the rooms including the hallway, next month I will pay you the balance of all I owe you."

I agreed to his request and for one extra day, we made as much money as any person could earn in one month, working six days a week. Probably Pavel heard how much I got for one day. When I got the money, I told him, "Pavel, you told me if I would pay you $2.50 a day, you would be satisfied. Very few people make that much. Here is your money— $5.00 a day! Are you happy?"

"No," said Pavel.

"Why?" I asked. "Isn't that enough?"

"Yes, but you are going to get much more," he sulked.

Pavel was jealous! Probably John had been right about him after all.

I told Pavel, "I am very sorry, but I don't want you to work with me any longer because of your attitude."

I loved Pavel because he was a very dedicated Christian, and his testimony was very powerful, but the devil tempted him in this love of money. I felt very sorry for him because he turned pale, but he wanted to get more than twice as much as he required at first during his work with me. Pavel had been able to buy a beautiful suit, a winter coat, and all sorts of things while he worked for me. He had helped his family and had saved some money in the bank.

My work went very slowly again. There was no glass or plaster work for about three months. In that time, John and I worked only four days. One day I was going home after work. It was about half-past five in the afternoon. A neighbor of mine called to me, "Jim, hurry up! Something has happened to your mother."

I ran into our home, went into the kitchen where my mother's bed was, and found her lying there, her face very sad and her mouth twisted. I heard her soft voice whispering, "It is finished."

My heart sank, but I smiled at her. "What happened, Mom?" I gently asked.

"I am paralyzed. Look at my left arm and leg," she gasped. She could hardly move them.

"Mother, don't worry. We will pray. Our God is great and He is able to perform a miracle," I told her.

I loved my mother very much. Now she had had a stroke and praise the Lord, it had happened in the right side of her brain, so that the left side of her body was paralyzed instead of the right one. The doctor explained that she was lucky because the function of the heart in the paralyzed area would help her to recover much faster.

I called my brother on the phone. The next day, he flew from the capital of Bulgaria, which is Sofia. He came into the bedroom where I was, and I cried for the first time since I had become a grown young man. Then I wiped the tears, swallowed my sorrow, and we both went to the kitchen to see our mother. We smiled at her and again encouraged her. My older sister came the next day. My younger sister was living with us in the same apartment with her husband and little daughter. Again we were together, all as a family, except my father. All of us encouraged our mother and prayed for her. I massaged her arm and leg according to the instructions of the doctor, and she began to recover. Then she was able to walk a little bit.

I took a job for an engineer until my own business picked up. Finally, I found some plaster and a customer. Just when I began to work, my engineer boss came into the apartment building.

"What are you doing here?" he asked me in a rough tone.

"I am making plaster ornaments," I replied.

Don't you know that private business is not allowed in our country?"

"Yes, I do. Still, I am doing it because in three months, I have worked only four days because of lack of glass. My mother is very ill in bed, and I desperately need money."

"I don't care," said my boss. "I'm going to take you to court."

I couldn't say anything. About five minutes later, he came back and told me, "Jim, I like you very much. You are my right hand. Always when I send you to any glazing job, big or small, you are there on time. So, I'll not take you to court, but stop working privately. The glass is coming any moment, and you are going to be all right," he assured me.

"Comrade Stoianov, may I quit working for the cooperative apartment building company?" I earnestly asked.

He was very surprised by my question and answered roughly, "Yes, you may."

"Thank you," I said. "Good-bye."

I went home happy because I had gotten my boss's permission to quit. Once a worker accepts a job from a company, he is not allowed to quit by choice. He has to get the permission of the top boss. If he quits and does not have the proper authorization, the Communists stamp his working book with a paragraph that says he is not disciplined and does not have the right to go to another company. Just like slaves! A person cannot quit his job and cannot go from city to city without giving a report to the police regarding where he is going, the purpose, and for how many days. The Communists must know EVERYTHING about EVERYBODY! In every block, they have a person who is called the block representative— either a man or a woman who has a record book with the names of and information about all the people who live in the block. They are obligated to know the details of the lives of every individual and to give reports to the police. The private life is gone behind the Iron Curtain!

4

The First Step of My Escape

I took advantage of the positive answer of my boss, organized my luggage, took my mother with me, and by train, left my city and went to Sofia. We had to sleep on the floor of my brother's kitchen. I succeeded in saving some money and bought a bed for my mother, and I continued to sleep on the floor of the kitchen with my mother, who was very happy to have a bed.

Right away, I found a job as a glazier in a new, big factory that produced iron. My brother joined me, and we had to travel by bus a long distance, back and forth. It was very hard to go so far and to work in the most primitive way, but we had no choice. I lived for six months in my brother's home and then decided to move out because it was so inconvenient. I bought beds for my brother's home, made plaster ornaments for his ceilings, and then left. My mother didn't want me to leave because she felt safer when I was there. Still, she needed constant care, and my lovely sister-in-law provided that service.

When I moved out of my brother's home, I found a job in the heart of the city of Sofia. My brother continued working with me, and later on, John came from Burgas and joined me.

While I was installing the glass of the Czechoslovakian embassy in Sofia, I heard that the Bulgarians were building an amusement center in the city of Skopje, Yugoslavia. Im-

mediately, I applied to be a glazier and waited anxiously to
hear if permission to go would be given me. One day a Communist boss of mine approached me and said, "Jim, I like
your work very much and want you to go to Yugoslavia. Are
you a member of the Communist party?"

"No, I am not," said I.

"If you were, your going to Yugoslavia would be much
easier."

Because of that question, we understand how bad the
Communist law is. They are the only privileged ones, and
have an easier life. If I were a Communist! But because I was
not, it would be difficult.

"Still, I would like for you to apply," he added.

"I did already," I answered.

"Let us go and check to see if you have been given permission, because we desperately need your help in Skopje!"

He got into his car and I took the tram. When I arrived, he
was waiting for me in front of the administrative building.
Inside, the clerk began to look for my name among many
applications.

"No, Comrade Dimov doesn't have permission from the
militia [police]."

My boss didn't like the answer and neither did I.

I thought, "I have missed the boat."

"Would you like to check that out again more carefully,
comrade?" my boss asked the clerk. And he checked more
closely this time.

"Here it is," said the clerk.

My heart jumped. To go to work in Yugoslavia—oh, what
a privilege! I went home happy and told my mother and the
rest I was leaving for Yugoslavia. My mother didn't like the
idea. Always, like every mother, she wanted to have us
around her.

For the last time, I had the opportunity to glorify the name of Jesus in my own language among my Christian brethren, when I praised the Lord for my salvation and everything He had done for me. Then I asked the Christians to pray to the Lord to be with me, to give me wisdom, and to use my life for His glory.

"I am leaving Bulgaria in a few days, and I would like you to remember me in your prayers."

After the service, everybody came to me and asked me where I was going.

"To Yugoslavia, to work as a glazier," I told them.

They couldn't believe it—a Christian going to Yugoslavia to work!

"It is something unbelievable!" they said.

Why not? ". . . with God all things are possible" (Matthew 19:26).

A few days later I left my brother's home, where I had my luggage organized. My mother was the only one standing on the front porch. She waved to me and cried. Probably she sensed that she would never see me again.

I was leaving my mother, my relatives, and my country—my people, my Christian brothers and sisters, but NOT God. Dressed nicely, slender and young, I was walking with big steps forward when I turned back for a last look at my mother, smiled, and waved to her. Rivers of tears flowed down her cheeks while she stretched her beckoning hands toward me, because I was not yet very far away. Her sincere mother's love was pulling me back, but the love of God, which is above all love and was in my heart, was pulling me forward to do the will of my heavenly Father.

My heart was beating very fast. Jesus Christ said, "And he that taketh not his cross, and followeth after me is not worthy of me" (Matthew 10:38), or whoever is not willing to give up everything for Christ's sake is not worthy to be His disciple. I was attracted by the love of Christ, which was much stronger than my mother's love. Not the Iron Curtain, nor the devil himself, nor my mother's love could stop the Lord's plan for me. Like wax under a clear, sunny day, my heart was melted under the strong heat of the love of God.

Dear Reader, if you are not comfortably warmed by the love of God, wake up! Tomorrow could be too late. Get a Bible, which is so available in the free world. Read it honestly and ask God to reveal Himself to you by asking the Lord Jesus to come into your heart. After you accept the Lord as your personal Saviour, you will be the happiest person in the world.

Full of the love of the Lord, rejoicing in His Spirit, I was leaving Bulgaria for Yugoslavia. "Lord, here am I—entirely in Your holy hands and perfect will. Lead me and direct me. Give me an opportunity to become a missionary and to be able to do something for Your Kingdom. My future, O Lord, is hidden in You, and because You are unlimited in love and power, stretch forth Your mighty hand and show me Your Way. Lead me, O Lord, and I will follow You."

I was so involved in my communication with the Lord, so strongly attracted by the future of my missionary activity that, just like a dream, in no time I found myself at the railroad station in Sofia. I felt very important and well dressed. With my big suitcase, I walked among many travelers. I was rushing into a new phase of my missionary journey. My need to escape was desperate. I was still in Bulgaria and at any moment the Communists could change their minds and give a new command to spoil my dreams. That made me more conscientious. I tried to be as relaxed as possible. Actually, I was very excited and joyful. I was anticipating and sensing the sweetness of being free in the near future. Yet I tried to look as cool as possible, so as not to give any impression of doubt among the servants of the devil, the Communists. I was trying to make sure nobody would have an opportunity to pull me by the collar of my coat and at the last minute tell me, "You are not allowed to leave Bulgaria."

Have you ever had the opportunity to watch a wild bird which has just been captured and put into a cage? My condition was the same. Finally, I was settled in my compartment with a few other passengers, anxiously waiting for the train to start. Within myself, I was praying and quietly asking God to open the way for spiritual blessings and to lead me and direct me according to His perfect will. I was wondering how all this could be! With so many thousands of glaziers in Bulgaria, how had I happened to be one of the two sent to Yugoslavia? The hand of the Lord surely was involved in everything concerning my life.

The conductor gave the signal and the train began to move slowly, steaming and making all kinds of noises like a big monster. My heart was beating very fast. I watched many people waving to their relatives and friends. I had nobody to wave to me; yet, I was the happiest of all! The train was moving faster and faster until I was not able to see the city of Sofia anymore.

Because of the high speed of the train, the houses and trees were blurred as we sped by. About two hours later, I saw the border between Bulgaria and Yugoslavia. So far as I can recall, it was April 5, 1965 when I arrived in the city of Skopje, Yugoslavia. The picture I faced was very pitiful. Many buildings had collapsed to the ground because of a big earthquake. Many countries were involved in helping to restore what had been damaged. Bulgaria was supposed to build an amusement center where I worked as a glazier. The other glazier was a retired pensioner but he was my boss because a Communist friend of his placed him there. He was not experienced as a glazier so I had to do the main work and he turned out to be my helper, but he received most of the money! I was not jealous at all, but happy and privileged to be able to work outside of Bulgaria. No Communist commanded me to go to Yugoslavia, but God had helped me in a special way.

It took a few days for me to adjust to the new circumstances. Some barracks had been built in which we were supposed to live. Almost all night long there was noise, especially Saturday and Sunday nights. All kinds of people from all over Bulgaria were there to work on the building. All of them were ungodly and drank a lot. It was unbearable to hear their immoral stories and to breathe air loaded with poisonous fumes of cigarette smoke and alcohol. Many nights, I couldn't sleep because of all kinds of fights and quarrels between different people. I tried to keep the window next to me open in order to get a little fresh air, but usually someone else would close it, and I had to bear the stench. One night, everything seemed quiet and I had just relaxed and had almost fallen asleep when I felt a gentle touch on my neck. I thought somebody was playing a trick on me. I moved to show I sensed the gentle touch and found that a four-legged little creature had used my neck as a platform, and jumped away in order to protect its life when I moved. It was a little mouse! A lot of mice invaded the new barracks because the men were hiding food in their bedside tables. I couldn't tolerate the mice, which were worse than anything else.

Again God helped me. Not far from the barracks I was in, I found a very old barracks built by the Germans during World War II. It had been completely neglected; it was very dirty and locked. I broke in and cleaned one of the rooms, then acquired an old bed and made a strong lock on the door. All alone there, I was very happy to be able to read my Bible, to pray, and to study English. Others became jealous of my privacy and caused me a lot of trouble. But God was with me all the time and was taking care of all my problems.

I was very anxious to explore the spiritual life in the city of Skopje. On the first Sunday, while walking on a street which led to the center of the city, I went a long distance and couldn't find a church. Because I was very tired from the long walk, I decided to go back to my new home, the old German war barracks, and to continue to study my new language. On the way home, I saw a sign in plain Bulgarian words: PRAYER HOME. My heart jumped! In a few minutes, I found myself in a small Methodist church. Very few people were there. The pastor was preaching in almost pure Bulgarian. He also preached in German because there was a group of young German boys and girls there. The Christians were very sincere and zealous in spreading the Gospel. After the service, some of them surrounded me and asked me all kinds of questions. I sensed a real brotherly love among them. One of them, whose name was John, became a good friend of mine.

John had a lovely wife and one child. He dearly loved the Lord. It was almost impossible to see John without a broad smile stretched all over his face. He looked a little bit like John Kennedy. One Saturday evening, I attended a Seventh Day Adventist church. There were many people standing around after the service. Somebody tapped me on the shoulder and called me "brother." My heart leaped with joy to see my new friend John, smiling as always. For the first time in a foreign country, I was called brother! That fact warmed my heart. In my church in Bulgaria, all of the Christians who dearly loved the Lord never failed to call each other brother and sister.

At that time, John won my confidence and became my best friend in Yugoslavia. He invited me to his home and treated me like his own blood brother. His wife was very kind and his little four-year-old daughter also became my friend. Later on, I found a Baptist church which was very small but also had very warm people. The Christians from the Methodist and Baptist churches were fellowshiping and visiting back and forth in their services. One day, I saw an American missionary evangelist in the Baptist church. He was visiting all denominations and was a very dynamic preacher. As he preached, he moved from one end of the platform to the other, making all kinds of gestures with his hands. After the service, I approached him very quietly and exchanged a few expressions in English. He was not very willing to talk to me. Maybe because of my broken English, he was trying to escape the conversation.

"Excuse me, sir! May I ask you something?" I asked.

"Yes, you may," said the tall, white-haired, American head of a mission in California.

"Would you give me your advice?"

"Of course," he answered. "Indeed, I will."

Then I said, "I want to be a missionary. Is there any way you can help me in that respect?"

"I am not Uncle Sam," was his cold answer, and that was the end of our conversation. I left him alone and continued to pray, not daring to share my dream with anybody.

One day, I was invited again by Brother John and in a special moment, I told him what was in my heart.

He said, "Let us pray, and if it is the will of the Lord, you will be a missionary away from your country. If not, you will try in vain to go to the United States of America."

I agreed, of course, because I can do nothing without the will of God! So I had a prayer partner for the first time in my life. And oh, how wonderful it was to have somebody to share and to pray with! The days went by and I continued to pray, work, and study English. I had been in Yugoslavia almost four months.

There are two ways to get rid of this evil system of rule

called communism. One is to die and the other is to escape. Being quite young, I did not want to die and so, I chose the second. Yet to escape is a great risk, and the Lord created the human being with a natural desire to live as long as possible on this earth.

5

The Miraculous Escape

Having a little financial help and a lot of spiritual strength, I contacted a very dear friend of mine who was willing to assist me in organizing my escape. We prayed together and the answer came. I was introduced to a faithful Christian who lived very close to the border between Yugoslavia and Greece, Bulgaria and nearby Turkey. He was very suspicious in the beginning and didn't have the freedom to negotiate with me. He wanted to make sure I was not a spy and that it was God's will for Brother Jim to go to America. In no time, we became good friends and he agreed to lead me over the border.

I had to return to Skopje in order to give the impression to the people who watched me that I was just a visitor in that area, so I boarded a bus for Skopje. There was a girl on the bus who knew me, so at the first bus stop in Strumitsa, I very carefully left the bus and when the girl was not looking in my direction, disappeared.

The faithful Christian brother was supposed to wait for me at the outskirts of a village that was located next to a mountain called Belasitsa. I was surprised when I found that he was not at the appointed place. I didn't get discouraged though, because I trusted in the Lord. Actually, I was constantly praying, but when I could not find him, I began to pray more fervently. I was in a border neighborhood and any moment, the Yugoslavian military guards could discover me and send me to Bulgaria.

Praying and waiting, I noticed a man riding nonchalantly on a donkey coming toward me. That man happened to be my dear friend, a young and very strong, healthy man. He arrived just about on time and greeted me in the name of the Lord. My cohort in the escape plan was the type of Christian who would sacrifice all to please the Lord or any one of His children. He also had a big heart. The first thing he did was to give me his Bulgarian Bible. (The people between Yugoslavia and Bulgaria speak almost the same language.) I thanked him for the most precious gift I had ever received. Still, I wanted him to keep his Bible because I knew it would be easy for me to get a Bible in any language when I got to the Western world. Besides, I had an English New Testament, which was given to me by a missionary in Skopje. My friend was happy to be able to keep his own Bible after all. Then he offered me some cookies, which I gladly accepted.

After a short conversation, he went back to take care of the donkey, which was making all kinds of noises, probably to make my escape more romantic. About an hour later, my friend came to me where I was waiting, behind a big tree. It was about 8:00 P.M. when my brother in the Lord arrived the second time. Of course, as born-again Christians, we decided to kneel down under the huge tree and pray.

I lifted up my head and said, "Lord, here I am—before a dangerous trip. If it is Your will, help me to cross the border. If not, stop me now. You have so many ways to help me or to stop me. And if I am to escape successfully, I would like to make sure I am under Your perfect will. I would like for You to give me a sign, Lord. As Your follower, I believe You are able to show me Your will by a sign. I want the sign to be a proof directly from You. I would like, Lord, to see the perfect Holy Bible number seven everywhere. I've chosen that number because I know seven is used from the beginning to the end of the Bible."

In researching the number seven, an American scientist with a Russian background proved the Bible to be the Word of God. It is virtually impossible to underline the number seven from the beginning to the end of the Bible. The Bible says, "For the Jews require a sign, and the Greeks seek after wisdom" (1 Corinthians 1:22). Being a spiritual "Jew" (and I'm sure all Christians are spiritual "Jews"), I desired to have a sign from the Lord. But as born-again Christians, we should never follow just signs, but also the Word of God.

When we finished our prayer, we got up, smiled at each other, and followed the Lord toward the border.

It was the twenty-first of September, 1965, at a little after 8:00 P.M. when we started the trip to the Greek border. I forgot about my request and everything else except to follow the Lord as He led. It seemed to me I was headed for an unusual experience—very exciting, very romantic, and very dangerous, but gloriously victorious. I was under very great pressure, and that's why I lost everything but my faith in the Lord, who was leading me to my most desirable and supreme dream—to be a missionary. Like the brightest star in my life, I was being led through the most dangerous (but guaranteed safe by the Lord) road in order to see my dream come true. My entire being was concentrated into one prayer to the Lord—that He make my escape successful so my dream would come true. I knew my journey was guaranteed because I was led directly by the Lord Jesus Christ. Yet, being a human, I had my thoughts flying around and around in my brain. A big storm welled up in the center of the ocean of my being, and the waves of the storm were higher than the mountain I was crossing.

It was a fantastic sight to see the huge mountain called Belasitsa separating several countries—Bulgaria, Yugoslavia and Greece! The entire mountain was most beautifully decorated with a natural green carpet made from bushes and trees. This was the view I had seen from a distance several days earlier. It was dark and we were climbing up the mountain under the green carpet. We held our breath as the dry, dead leaves crackled beneath our feet. Sometimes we would hear a resounding noise when our feet awakened some sleeping stones, and they began to roll down the mountain with great speed. Once we saw the figure of a man walking in our direction. We stopped moving to avoid any noise, which could attract the attention of the questionable person.

The darkness became more and more dense, and when the man disappeared, we continued our trip, full of the Spirit of the Lord and of a sense of hidden adventure. A little later, it became completely dark, and I lost my friend. Now what should I do? In which direction should I go? I could not hear any noise, which meant my friend was out of earshot. I could be captured by the Communists at any time! Oh, faith! Oh, sweet gift of God!

"Lord, You have the answer to this problem."

And here was the Lord whispering gently in my ear, "Call him; he is not far!"

"John, where are you?" I called as quietly as possible.

Right away, I heard his low voice and oh, how happy I was when I found him!

"Let's try to be as quiet as possible," he said. "At any moment, the guards could hear us and we will be victims in the hands of the Communists."

"Is it much farther to the border, John?"

"No. In just a little while, we will be there," he answered.

We had been groping along for about two hours, but it seemed like ten, to me. My friend told me it would take no more than two and a half hours, but that was not the case because of the unusual circumstances. At that moment, we were traveling through a very thick net of sticky, long plants. It looked as though we were stuck in a huge trap placed there by the enemy of our souls. Really, it was an unusual barrier of just a few feet of deep green strings. Any contact of the plants with our pants caused immediate sticking by the thousands of hooks of the plants, which gives them climbing capacity. Being more experienced, John went first, and I followed behind, trying to overcome the hindrance of the sticky plants and the darkness. In a hushed voice, I called to John again. He had disappeared into the thickness of the moonless night. A few minutes later, I was surprised to find him coming back, apparently searching for something.

"What is going on, John? Why did you come back?" I asked my Christian brother.

"I lost my hat," he whispered, "and we must find it! Otherwise, the border dogs will pick up the scent and will lead the Communists directly to my home. Nobody can fool a dog, and I don't want to continue until we find the hat."

I knew a well-trained dog could accomplish as much as eight experienced border guards. You cannot imagine how difficult it is to look for a lost hat on a very dark night in the thick underbrush, located in a very dangerous area—the border between the Communist and the free world. Oh, what a joy it was when we found the hat! I think it was easier to cross the sticky barrier than to look for the lost hat. Actually, having to stop and retrieve the hat was as hazardous as crossing the border.

Encouraged, we praised the Lord and thanked Him for helping us to overcome one obstacle after another. We continued our climb and after a long distance, we were still far from the border. I was extremely thirsty, tired, and a little discouraged because of the length of time it was taking. It already had taken twice the time my friend had predicted.

"Brother John, how much farther are we supposed to travel?" I queried again.

"We are very close to the border now. Would you like to go back to Bulgaria?" he asked.

"Oh, no! Let us continue the escape."

Now it was about 1:00 A.M. We saw a little light coming through the branches of the huge trees, from the moon, which was beyond the colossal body of the mountain. I could faintly see some trees, bushes, and even the face of Brother John. The illumination from the moon became more and more a threat to the possibility of my escape. Soon we could be exposed by the brightness of the moon and the Communists would see us immediately. I saw some dark clouds in the sky, and soon we saw the bright moon spreading its silver beams all over the area. All the trees, bushes, and grass were covered with sparkling silver reflections caused by the cold, white, and bright moon. We had to walk among thick bushes and underneath the shade of big trees. The beautiful view tempted me to go into the moonlight and shout out loud, "Blessed be the wonderful name of the Lord, my God, who created the mountains, the stars, the sun, and the moon." But my conscience did not allow me to do so because now was the time to praise the Lord quietly. Also, now was the time to ". . . be ye therefore wise as serpents, and harmless as doves" (Matthew 10:16). Even walking as quietly and secretly as possible, we couldn't avoid noise. We still had trouble avoiding the hidden stones under the dead, crackly leaves, which caused much noise. Suddenly, all the beauty of the view and charm of the surroundings and the romantic adventure of the great escape disappeared.

"Stop!" a loud voice pierced the air and spread deep into the far darkness. A clear echo resounded from the depth of the huge body of the mountain.

I thought, "This is the end of my earthly life."

We hid ourselves in a very thick bush, knelt down, and began to pray.

I was praying to the Lord and said, "Lord, here I am, facing the glorious door of death, which leads into eternal life in Your Presence. My greatest desire, Lord, is to let my beloved

Christian brethren know why I tried to escape. You know my heart the best, Lord. The deepest desire I ever had was to be a missionary. Lord, I would like my desire to be extended by Your putting the same burden in the hearts of others. Let them also try to escape and I believe some of them will succeed and go to the West to share our spiritual struggle and physical persecution with the Christians in the free world."

At that moment, my friend John whispered into my ear, "Are you afraid?"

"Yes," I answered, "because of you."

"Why because of me?" he asked.

"Brother John, you have a family—a wife and children. If the Communists catch us, your family is going to suffer. I am a single man and a foreigner here in Yugoslavia. If they kill me, I have only my relatives in Bulgaria to leave."

"Don't be afraid," Brother John whispered. "Have faith in God! Trust in the Lord!" He continued to encourage me. "If you want, we could go back. Would you like to go to Bulgaria?"

Quiet, but full of braveness, I said, "No, let us continue the escape."

"We could go back in no time," John said for the third time. Probably Brother John had a great desire to turn back himself, and join his family. Yet, he wanted to make sure we were in the will of God by asking me three times if I wanted to turn back.

"No, my brother! In spite of the circumstances, let us wait upon the Lord and continue to obey His perfect will under His present leadership."

My friend John was amazed at my courage, which undoubtedly came straight from the Lord. Yet I know what it means to be in the hands of the Communists. There is no mercy in any Communist heart. The noise became louder and louder. It seemed to be coming nearer and nearer to our hiding place—the bushes, which were protecting us. Actually our protection was the Lord Himself!

As suddenly as the loud noise of voices started, it stopped. (We continued to pray and urgently ask the Lord for a miracle.) We wondered if the guards had gone back to their guardhouse, since it became so quiet, but we sensed something or someone was still nearby. Suddenly, to our astonishment, we could faintly detect the sound of trained guard dogs quietly circling our hiding place, sniffing furiously, trying to find a scent. But alas—all was in vain because the miracle we had prayed for so desperately, the Lord had granted us. Just as the Lord shut the mouths of the lions for Daniel (*see* Daniel 6:22), so did He cut off the dogs' keen sense of smell for us.

Who can escape a bloodhound on his trail? The border guard dogs were very well trained—even to sniff out their victims quietly.

One after another, the dogs left. We crawled out of our shelter very quietly and continued forward to more dangerous but glorious experiences.

Near the border, Brother John told me, "We are very close to the border, and we should be extremely careful because this is the final step of our trip."

It was about 2:00 A.M. and I became desperately thirsty. Nothing is worse than thirst in the life of any living being on the earth. Something like thick glue formed in my mouth. My throat was very dry and every time I tried to swallow, the thick glue in my dry throat caused a sharp pain.

"Are you hungry?" Brother John asked.

"No, I am not hungry, but extremely thirsty, and it is very hard to bear."

"Have a little more patience, Brother Jim," my friend encouraged me.

The bright crystal moon looked through the dark clouds

and we could see very far. Yet, we had to hide ourselves and walk under the shade of the trees and bushes in order not to be seen. Suddenly, I saw a little house made out of bricks. Brother John explained that this was where the border guards stayed. It was built next to the very border between Yugoslavia and Greece, and we had to pass close to the guards' little house.

"Isn't it dangerous to cross the border so close to the guards, Brother John?"

"Just trust the Lord, brother. Let us continue to walk quietly and slowly."

Now we were facing the most dangerous moment of my escape. The border was a very long area—between thirty and fifty feet wide where there were no trees and no grass. The dirt was turned over in order for the Communists to recognize the footprints of anybody who crossed the border. The little house was about seventy or eighty feet from us, and we had to walk side by side as one person. This was a request of Brother John and he was so right. I agreed and took the side closest to the little house, which was on our left. Brother John was on my right, and we walked together like one person. If any guard fired a gun, I would be killed first. Brother John was in this predicament because of me and he should have the opportunity to escape if possible.

We were stealthily crossing the border, just like cats pursuing birds, stepping very gently, quietly, and secretly. We were going into a new territory. My heart was beating very fast; my throat was hurting me badly and my strength was leaving me because of indescribable thirst. If the Lord hadn't given me spiritual and physical support, I would have fainted!

Praise the Lord! We crossed the border unharmed! (I'm sure the Lord made the guards sleep, as we literally walked right under their noses and they couldn't "smell" us.) Neither did the dogs bother us again, and only the Lord knows why. Maybe some of the guards took the dogs and went to patrol farther up the border. My personal conclusion is that the Lord provided the greatest miracle in my life because by all rights, there should have been guards walking around on patrol duty.

Although we managed to slip by the guards, we were still tense and very much aware of the danger around us. Once across the border, Brother John said, "This is the country of Greece," and he made a sweeping motion with his hand toward the length and breadth of the border.

Now we had to separate. We embraced twice and kissed each other twice. It was 3:00 A.M. but still quite dark. All together, it had taken seven hours instead of two. I thanked the Lord and Brother John.

He said, "May the Lord always be with you and bless you and use you for His glory."

"Good-bye, until we see each other again, here on the earth or up in heaven, Brother John."

He went back to join his family, and I continued my trip alone, with the Lord.

6

Beyond the Mountain

Never before was I so exhausted, sleepy, and thirsty. My throat was not only parched, but it felt like I had a hard pipe between my throat and lungs. I walked on for a while and felt like collapsing for lack of strength. Finally, I lay on the ground and nearly fell asleep. It was extremely dangerous to sleep next to the border. Many times escapees like me were discovered by guards and dogs and taken even from a foreign land and put in prison or killed. So I got up and walked a little longer, stopping to rest again until I felt I was again falling asleep. I got up and continued my escape. When I was sure I was far from the border, I took a longer rest and said to the Lord, "Lord Jesus, I am dying for water. If this continues for a few hours, I won't be able to bear it. My Father, help me to find water. Yet, not my will but Thine be done."

And oh, how fast the Lord is to answer our prayers! He has so many simple, understandable ways to help us. He impressed me to cup my hands in back of my ears, and of course, any noise was then magnified. I was amazed to hear a low, bubbling sound of water somewhere in the distance. Immediately, the need for water drew me in that direction. Encouraged, I began to praise the Lord and thank Him in advance for helping me.

The sound of the bubbling water attracted all my being, as if I were a thirsty male deer. As the Scripture says, "As the hart panteth after the water brooks, so panteth my soul after thee, O God. My soul thirsteth for God, for the living God:

when shall I come and appear before God?" (Psalms 42:1, 2).
So my physical body was thirsting for water. Never in all my
life had I been so thirsty. The desire to satisfy my human
need occupied all my heart, spirit, soul, and body. Every step
and movement of mine was directing me to the water. At the
same time, I felt my physical strength was leaving me more
and more. Any moment, I could fall down on the ground and
one of three things could happen to me: I could leave my
earthly body and go to be with the Lord; I could fall asleep
and the Communists could capture me; or I could be unharmed and restored with good health after a long sleep.

But the Lord had something entirely different from all of
my thoughts, because He gave me enough strength to continue my agonizing trip. I noticed the dawn appearing very
gently and as quietly as my escape. Little by little, I neared
the source of water and was able to hear very clearly the
gurgling of the spring. A little later, I was very surprised to
see a great, deep valley, which was indeed a barrier between
me and the water. It was impossible to cross the gorge, so I
had to change my direction in order to continue my physical
survival on this earth. I continued to walk to the left because
it was not possible to cross to my right. The desperate need
for water made me willing to do anything, even to risk walking through the "valley of the shadow of death."

It was about 4:00 A.M. when I arrived at a place where it
seemed possible to cross. The new surroundings brought
added hope to my heart. Now I was going to take a chance,
humanly speaking, to pass through a new barrier. I asked the
Lord for guidance, claimed my walk in the name of Jesus, and
took my first step. Immediately, I realized how dangerous it
was to walk on slippery ground made out of dirt and stones.
I looked down the valley and my hair went in the air. The
gorge was very steep, very deep, and all rock. Maybe because
it was still dark, I couldn't see the bottom of the valley, nor

could I see very far looking in another direction. Oh, how the deepness of this bottomless valley could scare and discourage a person without faith in God! How much more thirst, darkness, and slippery ground in the border area would I have to endure?

A fast decision had to be made because I was literally dying of thirst. My lips were cracking more and bleeding; my mouth and throat were as dry as rocks.

"Lord Jesus, I have no strength, no help, no hope to leave this place. You are my Strength and Help and Hope. I commit my life into Your hands," I cried to the Lord.

How quick is our Lord to answer prayer! He impressed me this time to dig the ground and make places for my feet. My right hand was carrying a black leather traveling bag full of English books, a dictionary, magazines, shaving equipment, brushes for clothes and shoes—and cookies! Yes, I had everything but water. Very carefully I bent down and found a place to put the traveling bag on the ground, then I used it as a support so I would not fall into the valley. With my left hand, I dug platforms for my feet; my right hand was the support of my body on the traveling bag. The first few platforms I made with not too much effort because I still had not reached the peak of my suffering, and my strength was still enough to make some movements. While digging, I dug out all kinds of junk, rotten branches of trees, and leaves. Very often, I dug out big round stones which began to fall down with very high speed and disappeared with great noise into the bottomless valley of death. I thought if I began to roll like one of these stones, I'd be torn to pieces and nobody would know what happened to me but God.

To go back would be more dangerous than to continue because of the risky turn I had to make. I passed almost half of the distance, which was about two hundred feet. Because of the hard labor of my left hand and the rude use of my fingers as a rake, I felt extremely weak. Any moment, I could lose consciousness and begin to roll down with great speed like one of the rolling stones, to a natural, bottomless grave. Probably all kinds of beasts and reptiles were waiting for my body as a delicious breakfast, but I believed the Lord my God would protect me from all evil, even from the beasts. He was able to protect me even during my rolling down the pit, like He protected Daniel from the lions in the pit. Suddenly, I felt sharp pain shooting through my fingers. I looked at them; they were all covered with dirt on which I noticed red spots of blood. It was pinching and painful, but I continued to dig, using my last strength.

Finally, I said, "Lord, I am losing my balance and I am perishing!"

It was like Peter sinking after a short walk on the water. Here, the faithful hand of the Lord stretched forth, lifting all troubles away and placing the Twenty-Third Psalm in my heart.

The fourth verse especially lifted up my spirit and my heart. Strength like a flooded river occupied all my being. O faith, O indescribable sweet gift! The power through simple faith in the Lord Jesus, coming by the Word of God—the Bible is stronger than any other power in all the universe. The Word of the Lord lifted up my heart and I continued to pray with my bleeding lips, to dig with my bleeding fingers, and to breathe through my dry throat. In a few moments, a little saliva started flowing in my mouth so my choking condition was relieved a little bit. I felt the power of the Lord come upon me, and my strength was renewed from above.

Little by little, with the mighty help of the Lord, I crossed the valley of death and took a little rest. Then I continued to walk back in the direction of the noise of the bubbling water.

The new circumstances were not much different from the past, but at least there was no valley of death anymore, and the darkness was not so thick, because of the coming dawn.

Instead of that, my thirst began to choke me again; that's why I began to quicken my pace. What a surprise! I saw a man in the far distance, and a little farther, a small group of people. Was this a dream or a mirage? Maybe the noise of the water was an hallucination!

"Halooo," I cried, to get the attention of the people.

"Alooo!" answered the echo to me. None of the group moved to pay attention to the thirsty male "deer."

"Halooo!" I cried louder.

"Aooo aaa uuu eee," replied the echo.

"Why am I looking for help from unconcerned people?" I asked myself. "Lord, I turn to You again to help me to find water."

I knew I had distinctly heard the noise of the bubbling water. The closer I walked toward the source, the more I heard the sound of the water.

"It is real! There is bubbling water very close!" I was convinced. "Thank You, Lord, for answering my prayer."

More strength was poured into my body, and again I became more alert. In about ten minutes, I saw an unusually beautiful view; it was not a mirage—a few trees, a few big and many small stones among which I found a geyser of mountain water. Now I knew it was real, for sure, because I not only heard, but saw it! A big horizon was spread in front of me, covered with trees, grass, dead leaves, and stones.

I began to walk slowly and took a deep breath, which caused pain in my throat. I tried to sing and praise the Lord and that caused pain in my throat and lips, too. I stretched the fingers on my left hand and felt pain shoot through them.

"Lord, thank You for the pain," I said.

And then I went to the water, but I didn't drink right away. The utmost desire I had was not to satisfy my physical thirst but to praise the Lord and thank Him for helping me to escape.

There was a round stone, two yards in diameter. I chose it

as my prayer altar, knelt on it, raised my hands in the air, and
began to praise the Lord, to glorify His holy name, and to
thank Him for first leading me to the living water of life,
which is the Word of God. Of course, I didn't have much
strength to hold my hands in the air, nor to speak my words
out loud. I was just moving my cracked, bleeding lips and was
whispering gently to the Lord in one of the sweetest moments of my personal communications with my Saviour and
God.

When I finished my early-morning mountain devotion, I
lay next to the water and took a short rest. I didn't drink right
away because I was extremely tired and indescribably
thirsty. Many times, some runners who drink after a race die
because the body is not able to accept the water in an extremely tired condition. I was also a runner, although a different kind, and my conscience didn't allow me to drink immediately. When I felt rested enough, I went to the spring,
thanked the Lord again, knelt down, washed my hands, drew
a little water with my cupped right hand, and drank a little
bit of it like one of the soldiers of Gideon: "And the number
of them that lapped, putting their hand to their mouth, were
three hundred men . . ." (Judges 7:6).

Immediately, I was refreshed. Then I drank more water,
came to myself, and continued on my missionary adventure
trip. I was not only able to walk, but to run, if it were necessary—even to fly, if I had wings!

I had to cross many miles and many dangerous places. The
day was progressing with its sunlight and I could see very far
in the distance. Still, I couldn't reach the end of the mountain. Finally I saw a small road just wide enough for one
person to pass by. I noticed impressions of sheep and horses'
hooves. Following the winding road, it seemed to me there
was no end. The sun began to peek above the mountain and
a little later, smiled at me very gently. It reached first the

tops of the trees and later, most of the area was covered with its crimson beams. The view was captivating to the human sight, mind, and heart, to the extent of ecstasy. Every moment the golden light was occupying more space and was trying with all its power to scare the darkness of the night. The peaceful atmosphere was flooded with countless voices of carefree birds united in a huge natural orchestra, established by the Creator of the world.

I walked down and down the mountain and found more and more water. The beautiful sunbeams occupied all available spaces between the branches of the trees and when I was crossing them, it gave me the impression I was passing through a crimson curtain of beautiful cords, ropes, posts, and all kinds of figures made out of gold.

All at once, a very beautiful sight attracted my attention and in no time, I arrived at a small oasis with a few trees and next to the trees, a small natural water pool. I situated myself next to the little lake, which was about twenty or twenty-five feet around. Again I praised the Lord for helping me to escape, and decided to improve my appearance. I took off my clothes and washed my shirt and socks with soap and water. Then I spread them across a big branch to dry under the hot sunshine.

I used my sunglasses as a mirror to shave my beard and to see to wash my face with a lot of water, and smiled to the Lord.

"Alleluia! I praise You, Lord, for the victory in Your holy name."

I washed my feet, too. I would like to have taken a complete bath, but instead, I lay down on the ground to rest a little until my belongings were dry. In about thirty minutes, I was able to wear a clean shirt and socks. Then I brushed my suit and polished my shoes. I grabbed my black traveling bag and, like a tourist, continued my trip. When everything looked fine, a doubt (the most used tool of the devil) was brought to my mind—maybe I was still in Yugoslavia! It sounded so logical, so real.

I walked up and down, left and right, forward and backward. "It could be I'll never know for sure what could happen in my life," I said to myself.

One fact is always for sure—the Lord is with me, and He answers prayers. "Lord, help me to find out if this is the country of Greece." In no time the answer came.

Walking on a dirt road, going in a direction of uncertain destination, I noticed a cigarette box. I bent down, picked it up, and read the Greek letters written on it—the word *papastratos*. This should be the country of Greece, I concluded.

After all, I was going in the right direction. A little later, I saw some houses and a few people who were probably greeting me because they said something, but I couldn't answer because I didn't understand the language. To excuse my predicament, I pointed to my tongue with my finger. I could have given the impression they were talking to a dumb man.

Little by little, I approached a village until I arrived at a railroad station. I lay on a bench there and in a few seconds, fell asleep. Some noise woke me up, and I jumped with the thought that maybe I had missed the train. I was planning to take the train to the city of Athens and go to the American embassy to ask for political asylum, but the Lord had different plans for my trip. I tried to exchange some Yugoslavian money, but the people were not interested. A policeman came along and tried to talk to me, but that didn't work out. Then he asked me if I were a tourist. This word is international.

I answered, *"Ne,"* which is "no" in Bulgarian, but which means "yes" in Greek!

So we began to use the language of the hands. I began to

move my hands and explained I crossed the mountain and wanted to go to America. In other words, I was an escapee tourist to America. The policeman sent me to an army division where an army officer, through an interpreter, found out about the purpose of my escape. The interpreter was a Macedonian lady. The Bulgarian and Macedonian languages are just about the same. I explained how I crossed the mountain during evening and was very anxious to go to America, where I wanted to be a missionary.

The army officer ordered two soldiers to check me out very carefully to see if I wore a gun or concealed bombs, and then they drove me to the second largest city in Greece, called Thessalonica. One of the soldiers drove the jeep; the other one guarded me. In a few hours, we arrived in the city of Thessalonica, the same city for whose people the Apostle Paul wrote the Thessalonian letters.

Every moment was a new adventure because everything was so new, so interesting, and so exciting. I was put in the attic of a hotel, where I saw an Albanian family with two little children and a baby. Food was delivered to us for free. The Albanian man was very greedy about the food and always tried to get as much as possible. Often he had to throw the food away, but he didn't give up any amount. I tried to give part of mine to his family, and he still argued very often, telling me I received part of the food intended for his family. It was hard to live with a person who knew a little bit of English but argued and ate a lot. The conditions were very primitive and I felt very lonesome. In five days, I was sent to a special department where they took the impressions of my fingers over ten times. On the fifth day, I left by bus with a guard for a city called Kavalla.

7

In Prison

The city of Kavalla is located on the Aegean Sea shore in northern Greece. Most of the houses are white, and it is a joy to approach the city on a sunny day, as I did.

The man who was guarding me was very dark complected, wore sunglasses, and was very careful in his duty. He led me to the end of the city, where I saw big prison walls. It was unbearable to face the fact I was going to be behind the prison walls even just for a few moments. I was willing to go through any circumstances the Lord wanted me to go through; yet, I couldn't explain this fact. I was looking for freedom and ended up in a prison! My guard knocked on the door and a young man opened it. We went inside.

Behind the wall there was a one-story building and a few beautiful trees. The young man led me into the lobby of the primitive building, where I was asked to give up all my belongings and clothing including my New Testament in English, which was given to me by a missionary in Yugoslavia. A prisoner's suit was given to me which I didn't like at all but had to wear. One of the men took my belongings and another led me to my prisoner's cell.

"This is your room," said the man in plain Bulgarian. When I looked at the door, my heart jumped. It was cell number 7! Immediately there came to my mind the moment of my prayer before my escape.

I said to the Lord, "Thank You, Lord, for being so faithful to answer my prayer."

I entered my room, which was below ground level, and the man locked the door behind me.

Behind the door was written on paper in Bulgarian:

> Dear Escaper: Do not be afraid. You are under the free blue sky of Greece. Even if you are a Communist, just tell the truth and after a short period of time, you are going to be free.

Yet I was just like a bird which had flown out from the big cage of the Communists in Bulgaria (not a free country) and now was locked in a small cage in a free country! Immediately I missed my New Testament. For the first time in my life, I was without the Word of God and felt the spiritual thirst which is much stronger than the physical one.

"Lord, I miss Your Word," I began to pray. "Thank You, Lord, for allowing me to be in prison. Now I am dying spiritually and You are able to supply my spiritual hunger and thirst in the most miraculous way. You could drop me a complete Bible even through the ceiling of my cell."

The spiritual thirst is not only much stronger than the physical one, but it is a real starvation which leads to destruction of the eternal life of the human being. It is hard to comprehend that people have the Bible available and do not read it.

Food was offered to me and it was very delicious. I asked for a Bulgarian Bible, but I didn't receive it until I had struggled painfully within, for a while.

One week later, I was sent to cell number 3. As a Christian, I do not believe in numbers, but when the Lord wants to show me something, I believe everything. In my mind, I placed 3 next to 7 and it became 73. I thought, if I stay 73 days in this prison, it will be awful. At least once a week or every other week, I was called to one of the main offices and was asked questions about my personal life, family, and country. Some of the questions were political, concerning the military force in Bulgaria. I told my investigators I was not acquainted with any military situation in Bulgaria. I am a Christian and never was interested in politics. Still, the men in charge continued to question me and to transfer me from one investigator to another. Most of them spoke Bulgarian fluently. To one of them I said, "In Bulgaria, it is even dangerous to think about politics."

He was very surprised at the statement and asked me to explain why. "Because," I answered, "the time could come when a person could express his opinion and the secret police would get hold of him and then it would be hard to find out what happened to the poor citizen."

A few weeks later, I was allowed to go out for thirty minutes, later, one hour. A group of Bulgarians were allowed to get together and talk. There were always a few Greek boys around who guarded us.

The circumstances were unbearable in some respects. Worst of all was the fact that I didn't have a Bulgarian Bible. My spiritual struggle was indescribable and continued for twenty-four long days and nights. I was praying every day to the Lord to supply me with a Bible. The last day, I said, "Lord, I am dying spiritually! Give me, O Lord, the living water, the bread of life, because I cannot exist without the Word of God."

How good the Lord is! He had the right day planned for me. I didn't realize what was going on, and why I had to wait exactly twenty-four days for a Bible. On the twenty-fourth day of my imprisonment, I received a complete Bible in the Bulgarian language. I couldn't believe my eyes! It was like a dream. I couldn't read for the joy that was bubbling in my heart.

Because there was no calendar, or pencil, or anything to keep track of the days and months, every day I was marking a line on the wall with my spoon. I realized it was my birth-day when I received the Bible! Was it true or an hallucina-tion? Truly, it was real, praise the Lord! At last, I had a Bulgarian Bible in my hands. I am sure the Bible was not given to me as a birthday present because I know the Greek people do not like Bulgarians; neither do the Bulgarians like the Greeks. This is true about people of the world—not the Christians!

All the Greek soldiers at that prison were treating us in the worst possible way. They used to give us used razor blades and many times when I shaved, it caused tears to roll down my cheeks and mix with the soap on my face. Often I had to beg the boys to give me a newer razor blade.

In order to go to the bathroom, we had to ask permission; then we were allowed to go only once or twice a day. If I asked to go more than that, the guard got very angry with me without any reason.

The food was very delicious, but there was not enough. My bed had big bumps in it, and I tried everything in order to exchange it, but it didn't work out. These few examples give me all the right to declare the fact that the greatest gift I ever received was from God on my birthday, the gift which sweet-ened my life in prison—the Word of God, the Bible. My spiritual hunger and thirst were very strong. Ever since I can remember myself as a Christian, this was the first time I lacked a Bible completely. And now, here I was alone in my cell with the Bible in my hands, and it was not a dream but a fact.

I began to read the Bible from the very beginning and finished it in a very short time because I read all day long for about two weeks. Then I began to reread the New Testament again and again. From early in the morning to late evening, I was using the little available daylight coming from the very small window to read the precious, sweet Word of God. I began to memorize the Scriptures and to go deeper and deeper into the Bible—the greatest and bottomless ocean of the love of God.

The questioning continued and my investigators were not happy with the information I gave them. I began to witness about my faith in the Lord, but they were not interested. The days went by and I was very concerned about my mother. I wanted to send her a letter to let her know I was alive and healthy, but couldn't succeed. It was not allowed, and any communication with Bulgaria was forbidden. Every day, I could hear the turtledoves cooing early in the morning—the only announcers of the coming day.

On the seventy-third day (as I thought I would stay in prison), I was called for one last questioning. The Lord literally showed me that the seventy-third day was going to be the last day I would be investigated. A Greek man with straight, black hair and a rather heavyset build began to go over the papers prepared for me and again asked me political questions, and about my relatives, myself, and my country. He got irritated with me and tore up all the papers, and told me, "We can't get anything from you. Why don't you tell us something valuable? You are just like an overbaked lobster which doesn't give any juice. I tore your papers up, and in a few days you are going to be released from this prison and you will go to a small town called Lavrion, close to Athens."

"Thank you for your politeness, sir," I said, and left his office. I was anxiously waiting for the moment when I would be called and asked to get my belongings and leave the prison. On the seventh of September, exactly on the seventy-seventh day, I was released from the prison! All my belongings, including my New Testament in English, were given to me. I was praising the Lord for answering my prayer through the number seven. Two other boys were also released and we were sent to the small town of Lavrion.

We arrived in Lavrion and were taken to the disembarkment camp for escapees. People from most Communist countries who successfully escape are detained there to wait for their visa to go to the country they choose. The camp was not a palace—nor was it a prison, but just a waiting place. (Some people waited several years.) When I was established in a room, we became seven boys.

In the center of the compound, there was a large dining room which was used also for reading and meetings. I was very happy to find all kinds of American books and most of all, Bulgarian New Testaments. Everybody could take one for free. I couldn't believe my eyes. Free Bulgarian New Testaments! That was fantastic! I took one and began to read with thanksgiving in my heart. The Bible I received in prison was no longer in my possession because I had to leave it there. It is so wonderful to be free to witness for the Lord and best of all, to be able to offer a New Testament to anybody who is interested in the Word of God.

The first thing I did was to write a letter to my cousin in England. I asked her to send me some money because the food was horrible. Many times, the cook put roots in with the food and often we could find all kinds of junk in the meals. All of us made a petition to protest against the cook in order to get better food. We received an answer. The leadership of the United States Escapee Program (U.S.E.P.) couldn't do anything because the food was under the authority of the Greek people. When the cook learned about our petition, we discovered the food became worse. We saw that the main cook was selling the best meat as hot shish kebab and making money. Many times, he cooked beans with cabbage, which probably the pigs wouldn't eat because it tasted bad and there were stones in it. I had to work as much as possible to make extra money for food.

One day I made a little extra money and went to the

telephone company and asked to contact my older sister to describe my condition. I was very happy when the contact was made and I could tell my sister to talk to my mother very tactfully about me—that I was alive and healthy in the country of Greece. After talking to my sister, I felt a great relief in my heart because I was able to give her a message about my whereabouts and condition.

Finally I received a letter from my cousin. I was so happy when I got the letter, and opened it with trembling hands and began to read the sentences very rapidly. She encouraged me, in the beginning of the letter, to wait and to have patience. When she was in Bulgaria, I had told my cousin some young boys succeeded in getting to France. She had said, "You go to France, and I'll come by plane and pick you up and take you to England."

And now, in her letter, she had written that she was not able to come. I was very disappointed in the last statement. If she would come, I thought, I wouldn't have to stay so long in Lavrion because she would guarantee everything, and I would not have to suffer under these primitive conditions. But the Lord had a better plan for me. I continued reading the letter and was happy to read that an English friend of my cousin's husband was going to visit me with his wife and would bring me fifty pounds English money. I appreciated my cousin's help. I would have some money to buy food for a while.

In spite of the circumstances, every day I had the opportunity to witness for the Lord and share with my fellow Bulgarians the Good News of the Gospel. Every day I went to the post office to get my mail, and almost all of my trips were in vain.

My mother's letters were the best. They were full of love, and gave me a longing to go back to Bulgaria. But it would be the end of my life because the Communists could hang me or it would be a life without any future; and worst of all, the end of my missionary dream! No, not my mother, nor relatives, nor friends, nor country, nor anything else was able to cause me to go back. As a bright star, my missionary desire was attracting me to the best country in the world, the United States of America.

I was very interested in my new language, English. I enjoyed reading the Word of God and witnessing to my new friends. I was studying new English words and learning sentences by heart. I began to imagine my life in America, but everything was just imagination. I pictured America to be entirely a Christian country, like the Communists were saying it was. A great interest was for me to approach the American life in advance by trying to read magazines and newspapers. I looked at the pictures and tried to place myself among the American people. Most of all, I pictured myself as a missionary among Christians from all denominations. I knew I would have difficulties and problems, but I was sure the Lord would turn all problems into projects and would take care of everything. I cannot imagine the condition of the people of the world who are non-Christians. How can they live without believing in the Lord Jesus Christ? How can they exist without eternal security of life after death?

The days were rolling by, one after another, hiding and revealing something for everybody. One day I went to see an American missionary and to visit a church which was very close to my heart. To my great surprise, the church was on a street called Iolo number 70, on the seventh floor! On my way back, I decided to weigh myself on a scale which I saw against a wall outdoors. When I arrived in Greece, I was seventy-four kilograms. One kilogram is a little bit more than two pounds. I stepped on the scale and was happy to see the hand point to exactly seventy-seven kilograms. Praise the Lord! Seven everywhere! Just as I asked the Lord before my escape, all was coming to pass. I was praising the Lord and rejoicing for His love, faithfulness, and thanking Him for the answer to my prayer. The life in the camp was not exciting and a person feels worn out waiting in very primitive circumstances.

8

My Trip to the United States of America

The time went by very slowly. Every day, I was anxiously waiting for good news about my traveling to the United States. One day, I was pleasantly surprised in the office of the camp when I received a guarantee by a sponsor, which I needed to get out of the camp. It was a lady of whom I had never heard. Usually Bulgarians sponsor Bulgarians; Russians sponsor Russians, and so on. I couldn't explain why I should have an American lady as a sponsor. A few weeks later, I received a beautiful letter from the same lady, Mrs. Patricia Young. Later on, she sent me a picture of her family and a little description of the Young family. I tried to answer her by using my dictionary. As much as possible, I expressed my appreciation to Mrs. Young for being my sponsor.

It was a lovely winter day around the end of January 1966 when I saw my name on the bulletin board. A group of boys and one girl were supposed to go to the United States. I couldn't believe my eyes and I couldn't bear the happiness. I began to jump and scream for joy. When? was the question! A committee from U.S.E.P. came from Athens. We were called for a short meeting, where we were instructed about our traveling to America.

"Could you tell us when we are going to leave?" we asked.

It looked like they were purposely keeping the date from us. Finally, Miss Simson, the head of U.S.E.P., announced the

date, which was the seventh of February. I smiled and almost
burst with joyful laughter, but I didn't. After the meeting, I
ran out of the office and, like a young male deer, sped
through the camp yard to my room, to organize my luggage
for traveling.

Within a week everything was accomplished, and the small
group of boys and one girl were ready to travel to the greatest country on the earth. I couldn't comprehend this great
fact in my life. After so many tests, tribulations, and dangerous risks; after so many years of praying, waiting, and hoping,
here I was, ready to go to America. When I was in Bulgaria,
I discussed with a friend of mine (who is right now in West
Germany) not only how to escape, but how to adjust ourselves to the new life. We came to the conclusion not to start
our life in the free world in a big city. First, we supposed we
should live in a small village in the United States and little by
little, we should approach a bigger village. Then a small town
next to a bigger town, until we are in a position to make a
living and be able to adjust ourselves to a big city. The life
in a big city (we used our imagination) is so complicated and
so fast that newcomers could fail in many ways and could
collapse because of the unusual and extremely advanced
techniques, highly developed standard of living, and the exclusive culture and intelligence. And now I was going to
travel and visit the greatest city in the world, New York.
Maybe I am dreaming, I thought. How could this be true?
Am I going to be a missionary? Maybe this is just an hallucina-
tion.

A few days later, a ticket was given to me and it was
number forty-seven. "Lord Jesus, who am I for You to pay me
so much attention?" I asked.

We were driven to a harbor called Piraeus, close to Athens.
It was a lovely, sunny day when we arrived at the harbor. A
huge white ship was waiting for us. The sunbeams were

sparkling on the shiny ship, obediently waiting to be loaded for a great commission. The body of the ship was conveniently located in the harbor and peacefully settled to take its breath for a very long trip through the restless Atlantic Ocean.

The ship was Italian, very attractive, clean, alive, and quiet. It was just like a smooth, fluffy, and shiny swan which was patiently accepting loads. People, like ants, were pouring into the body of the giant, looking for their cabins in which they would spend about two weeks. So we took the ship called the *Christopher Columbus* and in the twentieth century, we were going to discover America!

The ship began to speed toward the restless surface of the Atlantic Ocean. I went to the back of the ship and enjoyed watching the troubled water behind the sea vessel, which left a long, white strip in its wake for miles.

I saw some dolphins jumping above the surface of the water. It looked like they were competing with the ship or trying to reach some food, appearing above and then disappearing into the water. The first few days, everything was fine and everybody was happy. I wrote a letter to my mother during my trip. The weather was just beautiful, sunny and cool. Very often we heard announcements in Italian, French, and English. The food was delicious. The Italian seamen were very friendly, helpful, and kind.

Suddenly the gigantic ship was shaken, and a person could think an enormous whale had hit the body of the peaceful, smooth-moving swan. An urgent announcement made everybody fearful. All the people turned pale. Twice we were instructed about how to use the life jackets in case of a crash. The picture was changed completely. The peace and happiness disappeared from all the faces but one. These were the symptoms of a big ocean storm. The night spread its darkness all over the ocean and embraced the ship.

During the evening dinner, most of the people refused to eat. We went to bed but couldn't sleep. The ship was like a little board in the stormy, gigantic, restless Atlantic Ocean. All night long, waves twice as big as the ship were hitting the now not-so-peaceful swan without any sympathy. The ship was constantly unbalanced. Everybody got seasick and scared to death but Brother Jim. All the time, I had a good attitude and never lost my peace. Moreover, I was rejoicing and singing spiritual Bulgarian songs. My friends were wondering what was happening to me and why I was not scared. How could I be scared? The Prince of Peace lives in my heart. I shall fear no evil (*see* Psalms 23:4). If the ship crashed, no problem! I was not afraid to die! And I meant it. To me, death is the door to my eternal joy, peace, and happiness in the presence of my Lord. The storm continued three days and three nights. No damages were reported.

The passengers began to come alive again. Everything was back to normal. The ship again became a giant and was moving smoothly toward the New World. Early in the morning (after ten days of traveling) on the seventeenth of February, we arrived in Halifax, Canada, and stepped on the American continent. All of us ran like wild people out of the ship and got lost in the city of Halifax. It was softly snowing and everything was frozen outdoors. We went to all kinds of stores to see the products and like wild animals, were trying to smell and discover the New World. To our great surprise, we found out we were still on the earth! The people had two ears and one nose, just like us.

The time came to return to the *Christopher Columbus,* and now we were supposed to discover the United States of America. On the eighteenth of February, we arrived at New York harbor. I saw the Statue of Liberty and the big skyscrapers. It is not real! I thought. It can't be true! It is unbelievable! It is fantastic! Newcomers like myself began to ask each other, "Is this true or a dream?"

The ship was moving slowly, triumphantly approaching the great harbor of New York City, looking for the right location to unload the luggage and the passengers in order to take its breath after such a big fight with the troubled waters of the restless Atlantic Ocean. Many hundreds of welcoming people were stretching their necks to recognize the faces of friends or relatives. I saw a small group with stretched necks, standing on their tiptoes, becoming taller and when tired, shorter.

My sponsor, Mrs. Young, her husband, their two children, and a formerly sponsored Bulgarian recognized my face and began to call me by name and to wave at me anxiously. I waved back to them happily. I took my luggage, which was carefully checked at the customs department, and joined the group waiting for me. I was very warmly welcomed to the United States and invited to get into a white Ford station wagon. We left New York and went to Pennsylvania. During the ride, I had a chance to witness to the young Bulgarian man, who happened to be an atheist. My sponsor was curious to find out what we were discussing. She was very pleased to hear I was witnessing for the Lord.

Soon we arrived at the home of my sponsor in the city of Scranton, Pennsylvania. My sponsor told me, "Your room is upstairs."

I took my luggage and settled myself in a room which I was supposed to share with Krichi, a Chinese boy. I was very curious to find out if my number seven still was before me, as I had asked the Lord. I began to investigate my room and on one of the walls, there were seven pictures. In the pictures of six of them were painted seven bicycles. On the other wall, there were another seven pictures. In three of the pictures were painted seven singing birds. In my room, there were seven lamps, seven sitting places, and when I arrived in the home, we became seven people— Seven sevens!

Then I said, "Lord, that's enough. I am sure it is Your will for me to be in this country."

Just like the request of Gideon about the fleece in the Old Testament ("Behold, I will put a fleece of wool in the floor; and if the dew be on the fleece only, and it be dry upon all the earth beside, then shall I know that thou wilt save Israel by mine hand, as thou hast said" [Judges 6:37]), something in miniature had happened to me. How could I not believe in God? How could I stop praising the Lord for His love and faithfulness and mercy? All over the world around us and in us, there is undeniable evidence of the existence of God. The strongest evidence, however, is the personal relationship with the Lord. It takes more faith not to believe than to believe. How would a human being be able to afford not to believe? The animal knows its master, the human being does not know his Creator. How miserable is the condition of an atheist!

In a few days, I was accepted to work in a glazing company —but not to be a glazier as sponsored! For the first time, I had an American boss. He was a very kind man and never rushed me for anything. I found out that in order to work as a glazier, I had to become a member of the union of glaziers. I didn't mind going through any procedure and any job in order to get the right salary. The union representative told me I had to wait two weeks and then I would be accepted by the union. In the meantime, my boss asked me to paint the building in which we worked.

Two weeks passed and I asked the union representative, "Excuse me, sir. Would you tell me when are you going to accept me to become a member of the union?"

"Have a little patience," he answered, very relaxed. "In about two weeks, we will accept you in our union."

I got the impression that in America there is a saying, "in two weeks." I continued painting the building and receiving

$1.50 an hour instead of $4.00, as the rest of the glaziers received. At the same time, I was praying, asking God to change the circumstances, because I didn't get what I was promised, and I didn't see what I expected. I was expecting to see the owner hiring and firing the people—not the union having control and dominion. Naturally I had to pay room and board, and when the taxes were deducted, I had about $18.00 a week left in my pocket. I went to the store to buy a belt. It was $4.00. I bought a raincoat. I believe it was $20.00. Now I was wondering if this was really America. Maybe I was still dreaming.

One day, I took the bus and went to New York to look for my former Sunday-school teacher, Mary Zaplishnii. Of course, it would be a miracle to find a person in a city like New York. I didn't have any address or any information to help me. My Lord was the only One to follow because He knows everybody in the world, and He knows every direction. My purpose was not only to find her but to ask my former Sunday-school teacher for help. I needed money to buy a ticket to California. Since my childhood, I didn't like the winter climate. Now, again I experienced the cold weather. Whether I would receive help or not was another question!

I went to a fairly big church and decided to ask the congregation. It was a Sunday-morning service, and there were quite a few people in the church. The preacher was sharing, very effectively and intelligently, facts about the Word of God, the Bible. I couldn't understand everything, but I enjoyed listening to the preacher. Question time was given to the audience and I took advantage of it. I got up and asked if anybody knew a family called Zaplishnii. Everybody turned to me but nobody raised a hand. Then I explained as slowly and clearly as possible why I was looking for the Zaplishnii family. One of their daughters was my former Sunday-school teacher, and if somebody knew the name, I would appreciate some information.

A nice lady with a beautiful smile waved from the corner and said, "I know the family." She happened to be a missionary to China and because of her missionary activities was acquainted with the Zaplishnii family. A few ladies told me, "She is the preacher's wife."

I was very happy and patiently waited for the end of the service. When the Sunday-school service was over, the missionary lady came to me and introduced herself as the preacher's wife. "I am Mrs. Irene Brett," she explained. "The Zaplishniis are over eighty miles away from New York."

Her husband joined us and I asked if I could get the telephone number. We went to a telephone booth and found the telephone number through information. Brother Brett offered to drive me there. It was so nice of him to help me in that respect. I had a hard time accepting his offer; yet, I humbled myself, got into their car, and we left New York City for Wallkill, New York. When we were close to our destination, the road was very bad. Brother Brett said, "Even in the United States there are bad roads."

We traveled eighty-eight miles and arrived at the home of my Sunday-school teacher, Mary. She was very happy to see me. Her mother, Olga, was still well and had a very alert spirit. She was one of the strongest spiritual pillars of our church in Bulgaria and an example of one of the finest followers of the Lord Jesus. Sister Olga shared quite a few experiences of her spiritual life in Bulgaria. She asked me if I had gotten used to the American sandwiches. In Bulgaria, we are not used to sandwiches, but we enjoyed hot meals if we had the money to buy the ingredients to make the meals.

Mary was very surprised to see a young man over six feet tall instead of a nine-year-old boy, often ashamed of his dirty hands and dressed in a small jacket made out of used cloth, with shorts and torn winter stockings. She couldn't believe her eyes. The Bretts had to leave, and I thanked them very kindly. I explained to Mary my desire to go to California. My low income didn't give me a chance to make any money for traveling. I told her how much I needed her assistance in lending me the money just to buy my ticket to California.

I told her, "You are the only one I dare to ask for help. Immediately after I make enough money for the loan, I will send it back."

She promised to discuss it with her husband and would let me know by letter. Her husband was a nice young man with a lovely personality, very strong mentally, spiritually, and physically. He had a healthy, humble smile. I got a most wonderful impression of him. He drove me back to the New York bus station, gave me ten dollars, and went home to join his family. I went back to Scranton, Pennsylvania, and continued working and patiently waited for a letter from Mary. In about two weeks, I received the letter, opened it, and read it eagerly. In Bulgarian, Mary described their financial condition. Her husband had gotten sick and, to my disappointment, could not help me. I had to look for another outlet.

One day at work, the union representative came my way, and in spite of my decision to go to California, I asked him when I would be accepted as a member of the union.

"In two weeks," I heard the same answer.

"How many times do I have to wait two weeks?" I asked. "Your two-weeks' promises are endless."

"Have patience," the union boss told me. "It takes time."

I was wondering what happened to my guarantee to work as a glazier. I had to walk to work because there was no bus transportation that way. I was very disappointed because of all the negative results. Outdoors, it was very cold. When I was going home, I saw a sign: USED CARS. They looked brand-new to me. I was watching the people, the buildings, the life on my way to work. In spite of my disappointment, I was very happy because, after all, this was the United States of America, and I was very encouraged for the future.

Living in that little town made me think deeper. From one side, all kinds of barriers, including the language barrier; from the other, all kinds of goods and blessings in the near future. God was trying to show me something, to teach me something which I couldn't understand in the beginning. Later on, I got the answer: *Jim, My son, not your way but Mine is going to teach you a lesson. Jim, My son, I am building your faith and your character to use you the way I want, not the way you want.* The Lord was really working in my life, even by the negative results and disappointments. He was teaching me patience and humbleness through all the experiences, trials, tribulations, and tests. All are for good because God allows them.

One night after dinner, I went downstairs into the basement to wash a few pieces of clothing. Mrs. Young came downstairs and I told her about my decision to go to California. She didn't like the idea at all.

"I want you to stay here, Jim," she said. "You are going to learn English better and we would like to hear your testimony in our church. We would like to have you describe the condition of the people of your country and the Christian life there."

"No, Mrs. Young, I must go to California. I have a very ill mother and a blind friend without hands. I want to help them financially. How could I help them when I cannot take care of my own needs with this low salary?"

"Jim," said Mrs. Young, "the owner of the glazing company is fighting with the workers to accept you as a member of the union."

"Why is he fighting?" I asked.

"They told him, 'If the union accepts this foreigner, we will

MY TRIP TO THE UNITED STATES OF AMERICA

strike. We don't want new members. There is not enough work for us.'"

"Mrs. Young, I didn't come here to cause a fight. You did enough for me by sponsoring me."

"No, Jim. You must stay here. California didn't sponsor you."

"I do appreciate your sponsorship, Mrs. Young; don't misunderstand me. Yet, if you didn't, somebody else would sponsor me. I would like to ask you something; may I?"

"Of course," she said.

"Mrs. Young, do you love me?"

She couldn't quite understand my surprising question. I was not sure if I expressed myself correctly, so I made it more clear.

"Do you love me in the Lord, Mrs. Young?"

"Oh, yes, indeed," she answered.

"In that case, you should tell me, 'Jim, go to California, and may the Lord bless you abundantly!'"

"No, Jim, I want you to stay here. If you go to California, you are going to suffer. At least become a member of our church. The only requirement we ask of you is to believe in the Lord Jesus Christ. When the time comes to go to California, I will give you a letter of recommendation, and you will be settled in no time. The people of our denomination will help you."

"Mrs. Young, I thank you so much for your motherly advice and thoughtful suggestions, but I am not looking for sympathy. This is a fact, not because of pride, but because I've got what I was looking for. I was looking for freedom, and I have it. Now I would like to know if I am allowed to go to California."

"You are free to go to any state in America," she said, "but I want you to stay here. We need you for a speaker in this area. Our people need to hear from you, who came from behind the Iron Curtain. It will be very effective when you know English well enough to share in meetings about the life under the Communist system of rule."

How right was Mrs. Young and how right was the poor Bulgarian boy! She wanted to supervise my babyhood as an American, and I agree it was necessary for me. She was responsible because she gave me a guarantee, and with motherly advice, wanted to lift me up until I was able to solve my problems as a grown citizen of the United States. I wanted her to be free from responsibility and to let me fight by myself the raw reality of the beginning of my new life.

9

My Trip to California

I quit my "glazing" job in Scranton and went to New York to the same church, to look for the same preacher, Mr. Brett. He was very happy to see me again and invited me into his home. I told him about my decision to go to California. At a very convenient time, very tactfully, I approached him and asked him to lend me money for my plane ticket.

"Don't worry, Jim. I will help you," said Brother Brett reassuringly.

We went to Mr. and Mrs. Brett's Spanish-style home. He asked me if I could change the broken glass of the windows and paint the frames.

"I'll be more than happy," I answered.

In four days, I fixed all the broken glass, reinstalled the loose panes, and painted the frames. For this work, he paid me $50. I refused the money.

"Here is $153 for your plane ticket. When you make some extra money and you remember me, send $100 back. If you forget, no problem, no obligation at all." (After all, how beautiful it is to share a burden and to receive a response from Christians who truly love the Lord.)

"I am going to send you back $153, as I stated."

"You shouldn't, because you earned your $50," he said.

"I do appreciate your offer so much and will never forget your help," I replied.

Mrs. Brett made me feel at home in the most hospitable way, with a clean bed and delicious meals. Her smile and love impressed my heart as a foreigner in the sweetest way. She gave me the address of a missionary lady in San Francisco where I was supposed to live.

The next day, Mr. and Mrs. Brett brought me to the airport in Newark, and in the most loving way, they left in my memory examples of beautiful Christian lives. Mr. Brett hugged and kissed me as if I were his son. The love and help they gave me caused them to be the closest friends I ever had in my life.

I took a plane to San Francisco and was flying in a very modern jet across the United States. I was poorly dressed but very happy and even a little proud to fly in America, traveling to California. Oh, it was too much for me to remain humble. In five hours, I arrived in San Francisco. Then I took the bus and arrived at the home of the missionary.

She was very old and had a dog which shed its hair all over. I had to sleep in the basement in a small, moldy, and smelly room. My bed was very clean, so I was happy in that respect. The next day, I went to an unemployment agency to look for work. I filed my application, in which I stated not only that I was a glazier but that I would accept any kind of job. They promised to call me as soon as a job was available.

A new friend of mine invited me to a young-adults' meeting. There were about four hundred young people in a very big church. My friend introduced me to the young people by asking me questions—"What is your name? What is the name of your country, your church?" When I said the name of my church, a young woman about thirty-five years old said in a mocking way, "Aaaaimen!"

The auditorium was filled with loud laughter. I was shocked by their action. Is it wrong to be from such a church? I turned pale and faced the audience. At once they stopped laughing, and I sat down, brokenhearted. If I were wrong because of my church, where was the love and righteousness of them who laughed at me? If I were perishing because of wrong doctrine, where was the love of the laughing ones?

All of them but my friend and I, like sheep, followed the mocking tune of a foolish woman and laughed at the poor Bulgarian boy.

After that time, I never mentioned the name of my church again. I became interdenominational. If anybody asks me, "What is your denomination?" my answer is, "I am a Christian! I have no denomination."

In Bulgaria and other Communist-controlled countries, the denomination problem is nonexistent because of the persecution of Christians. All of us are leading people to Christ and not fighting to prove which denomination is wrong and which is right. Actually, to me there are no denominations or sects. These are steps of spiritual development. Some people are in a low spiritual standard of living; others are in a higher one, and others are in the highest and are at the top of the spiritual life of their country. If you think your spiritual life is above others, the worst mistake you could make is to put the people of different spiritual levels lower than they are. Build them up by adding your encouragement and your spiritual experiences in the Lord to make them grow higher even than your own condition. Precious brother or sister, ladies and gentlemen, precious follower of the Lord—from all steps of spiritual levels remember, the Lord wants us to be helpful hands to each other; not to destroy weaker ones, but to carry them on our shoulders like the Lord did with the lost sheep: "And when he hath found it, he layeth it on his shoulders, rejoicing" (Luke 15:5).

I was six days looking for a job all day long, every day, in vain. All over that beautiful city of San Francisco—unions, unions, unions! Since that time, I don't like unions at all. To people who belong to the union, it is all right, but outsiders are in a very bad position, especially when the outsiders are newcomers in this great country.

One night I was brought to another, more spiritual church, and I thought, "This is the place where I could share my testimony and feel like I am in my home church."

I was very happy when the pastor of the church said, "This is a testimony night. You could share what the Lord has done for you."

Quite a few people shared lovely testimonies. I got up and tried to describe in miniature my testimony. About three to five minutes passed and I was shocked again. The pastor cut me off just in the middle of my sharing. My heart was beating very fast, and I couldn't explain the reason. I realize my English is not very smooth, and maybe Americans do not like a foreign accent. But these people were Christians. They shouldn't have acted like that. I also know that it takes a little longer than usual for a foreigner. Still, they should have realized that I have a language problem. After the service, I thought the pastor would come to me and explain or apologize. He didn't pay any attention to me, as if nothing had happened. A young Christian came and introduced himself and explained the situation to me.

"Here in America," he said, "everything is very fast."

"Brother," I replied, "I didn't even talk for five minutes. Why should we be fast in church? Let us give the Lord a chance to control the speed, at least in church."

Again, brokenhearted, I left that church. In six days I couldn't find work or a home church.

There was a young Christian brother who asked me if I would travel with him to Los Angeles. I accepted the offer and the next day, we left San Francisco for Los Angeles. From a Russian church, I got the address of a Russian pastor in east Los Angeles. My driver brought me successfully to that address. I gave him some money for driving me and thanked him for being so very kind to me. About an hour later, the Russian pastor came and was surprised to see an uninvited guest waiting for him. I explained my condition and he said, "Brother, this key is your key. This refrigerator is your refrigerator. This bed is your bed. This home is your home."

"Oh, brother, that's too much to accept. At least keep the bed for yourself."

"No, I am going to sleep on the couch."

My heart was melted by his Christian love. I was in his apartment for two nights and one day. On the second day I found an apartment, which I rented without any deposit. The owner happened to be a Christian, so I lived there for over a month without paying rent until I had some money to pay my obligation. I was invited to the church of the Russian pastor and it was very nice to join sincere Christians. Some of them started to help me look for work; some gave me a few pots, dishes, spoons, and forks, so I had some kitchen necessities.

Two weeks later, I got a job in a Russian furniture-making factory. I began to work very anxiously in order to make some money to pay my first obligations. Some of the workers came to me and told me not to work so fast because the boss would make all of them work like me. I agreed and slowed down a little bit. The boss came and told me, "You work very slow. This old man, the janitor, does much more than you."

Of course it was not true because even working a little slower, I still worked faster than anybody else. I told him, "This is a free country, and if you don't like me, I will find another job."

"You are not supposed to talk like that in America," he said, speaking in Russian.

"Don't you see that I work faster than anybody else? Why do you require more?"

He ignored me and left. I was getting $1.65 an hour and was looking for extra part-time work. A few days later, I asked one of the workers if he could help me to find a part-time job because of my great needs. He happened to be a friend of my boss and reported to him about my request. Employees were not allowed to work any part-time job. A little before working time was over, my boss came and handed me my check and said, "You are fired."

I didn't understand his action, and told him, "In this respect, you did worse than the Communists would do to a worker. At least they warn you two weeks in advance. If I did something wrong, tell me, please."

"That is the end," he said, and left me without explanation. A friend of mine asked him, "Why did you fire him?"

"Because he was looking for part-time work," he answered.

"But he is very poor," my friend explained. "He doesn't have money to buy food."

For three nights and three days, my Russian boss could not sleep and eat because he fired a poor foreigner; probably because he had experienced what it means not to work, not to have relatives, and not to understand the language of the people you are living and working with.

A Russian Christian brother helped me to find another job in a trailer-making company, where I would make $1.85 an hour. I worked in the insulation department, then in the plumbing department, and as a carpenter, too.

My new boss was very pleased with my work, but a few weeks later, I quit my job there and moved to Hollywood to work as a painter for a Bulgarian man.

I was very excited about the new job, hoping to get a higher salary. How much I would get, I didn't know in the beginning. I was advised not to ask the new boss because he would get angry. At the end of the week, the Bulgarian painter told me my salary would be $1.50 an hour. I was very surprised by the offer. He became angry with me and said, "I'll pay $2.00 an hour, but you will not work for me any-more."

He thought I'd be scared and accept the $1.50 an hour. I told him even $2.00 an hour was very low, considering my ability as a painter. I had saved enough money to buy a 1959 Oldsmobile. The next week, I applied to work for a big glaz-ing company in Los Angeles, where I was accepted and was given $4.99 an hour. I had to pay $80.00 the first month, which was part of the total of $350.00 which every member had to pay to the union. It was promised that I would be accepted as a member in the union after the total amount was paid. I found a part-time job as a painter in the building where I lived. One month later, I was laid off by the glazing company. A week after that, I was called to continue working as a glazier and two weeks later, laid off again. I was never called back. At that time, two hundred glaziers were laid off. I continued to work independently as a painter.

With very hard labor and great economy, I saved some money and sent Mr. Brett $153. Two weeks later, he sent me $50 back and explained it was for my labor in his house. I continued to work very hard, and saved every penny. At the same time, I never failed to pray to the Lord to make my dream come true. The desire to be a missionary never dimin-ished. On the contrary, it grew bigger and bigger. I saved some money and bought carpet-cleaning machines and a little later, an upholstery-cleaning machine. I began to ad-vertise my new business from door to door.

One day I was almost on the border of despair. I couldn't pay my rent; other bills came and I felt very miserable. I began to pray and cried out before the Lord. That day, I distributed over one hundred brochures. It was late in the afternoon when I came to my apartment, completely worn out physically and exhausted mentally. Still, my spirit was quite awake.

I took my clothing off and collapsed on my bed. In about forty-five minutes, I got up, dressed, prayed again, and opened the door to leave for my door-to-door distribution of my carpet-and-upholstery-cleaning advertising brochures. At that moment, my telephone rang and the manager of an Indian church told me he was very interested in my new equipment and he would like me to go and give him a free estimate. I was very happy to do so and went immediately. I gave him a very reasonable price for upholstery-and-carpet cleaning. To my greatest surprise, in one hour I cleaned the upholstery of a little shrine, and I made $68. The next day, the manager sent a free helper to me who moved the chairs and in seven hours, I cleaned the carpet and made $80—$148 all together.

I paid my rent and bills immediately and was very happy. Little by little, I got more customers and was satisfied for a while. My new business was up and down many times. One day, I needed to pay a bill of twenty dollars. I was asking the Lord to help me, and the answer came. I was coming back from a young-adults' meeting at a nearby church. On the sidewalk next to the entrance of the parking lot, I thought I saw a one-dollar bill. When I picked it up, it happened to be a twenty-dollar bill! How could I stop praising the Lord for taking care of my needs? Exactly as much as we need, He is providing daily.

One day I was driving in Hollywood and I saw a sign on a house: FOR SALE. I looked at the house and liked it quite a bit. I didn't want to deal with a realtor and decided to leave. Just as I was getting into my car, an elderly lady called me and asked if I were interested in buying the house.

I told her, "Yes, I am, but I don't like making a deal with a realtor. I am looking for a private party."

"Don't pay any attention to the sign," she said. "It has been here longer than the contracted time."

She went to the sign, pulled it out, and threw it away. "Now, do you want to see the house inside?"

"Yes, I would like to see it."

The house was very dirty, covered with loose wallpaper in many places. The walls and the light fixtures were all covered with nicotine stains.

"Sit down," she invited me kindly. "Do you like the house?"

"Yes, I do. How much is it?"

"The price is $35,000."

"Oh, that is too much for me."

"I'll give it to you for $33,000 because there is no agent."

"Is this the final price?" I asked.

"No, you could pay me $30,000," she said.

"No, I can't," I answered. "It's still too high for me."

"How about $28,000?" she asked.

"I am willing to pay $27,000."

"That's fine," agreed the lady.

Isn't that a miracle! I was looking for a house without any money for a down payment. A neighbor told me that originally the lady wanted $49,500, and now she came down to $27,000—and I was making a deal without any money. How great is God! I know my Lord is able to provide a miracle anytime. I borrowed the money from friends and put $2,700 down for the house.

10

Shirley

I had three months' escrow until the house had to be transferred to my name. The Motor Vehicles department from Sacramento sent me a letter because of an accident I had been in, and they required a $2,480 deposit in order to save my license. All the people except the elderly lady who caused the accident turned against me through their insurance companies. All the damages were required from me because I was the last in the column of cars in the accident. And, worst of all, I didn't have any insurance. In no time, I contacted some faithful Christian friends who lent me about $7,000, which I soon returned with 10 percent interest. It took me about a year to pay everything back.

When I got the keys to the house, I couldn't believe it! I opened the front door, went into the living room, into the dining room, into the kitchen, into the downstairs bedroom. Upstairs, there were four more bedrooms—I got lost! Five bedrooms, three bathrooms, all kinds of rooms! Was this a dream or reality?

I dedicated my home to the Lord. Yet, I was not happy in the respect of my supreme desire—to be a missionary. I began to paint and fix up my house little by little. In the backyard, I found two lemon trees, one pineapple tree, a big apricot tree, and quite a few rose bushes, which were growing along the south hedge-fence of the lot. I began to water the neglected trees and plants. Little by little, everything was restored.

Some furniture was left for me, including a stove and a refrigerator. I began to investigate the closets and found about ninety dresses and all kinds of old-fashioned pictures and articles. My house happened to be a gold mine. The garage also was full of tools and other useful objects. Many thoughts and memories came to me about my past. I pictured myself with my short pants and long stockings going to school absolutely hungry, watching my friends eating their sandwiches while my mouth watered. Now I had not only freedom, but my own business and a private house. What a love of the Lord!

I was invited to quite a few churches to share my testimony. Personally, I was blessed anytime I had that great privilege—to fellowship with Christians. Many times, they collected love offerings, but I refused to take them. Once a Christian brother from a Baptist church received the love offering and literally forced me to take the money by putting it in my pocket. I explained to him, "This is God's money; and besides, I am working."

Nothing could convince him to take the money back. "It is yours," he stated, and changed the subject of the conversation.

I continued to pray patiently before the Lord to bring my dream to pass. At the same time, I wanted to get married. I was not nearly great enough to sacrifice my life completely as did the Apostle Paul. I was looking for the right life-partner very actively and very carefully. Some friends introduced me to quite a few attractive young ladies. They were very nice and very modern. I was raised in a very old-fashioned community, and the natural beauty of a young lady had to win my heart.

I was going from church to church all over Los Angeles to get my spiritual food by hearing different preachers, to get an idea how the Americans serve the Lord, to fellowship with the Christians, to praise the Lord, to share the Christian life behind the Iron Curtain, and to share my personal testimony. I was also looking for the right young lady to become my life-partner. Many girls didn't like me. Maybe they were blind. I didn't like many of the girls, either. Maybe I was blind.

My business was slow and I had plenty of time to pray, to read the Bible, and to look for a girl friend. The time was flying by very fast and I thought probably I should go to Europe to look for the right girl. American girls are very beautiful but too modern for me.

A friend of mine, upon my request, gave me thirty or forty names, addresses, and telephone numbers of girls, so I began to act by calling them. It didn't take me much time to check out almost all of them. With some, I finished over the telephone. Some I met and was very disappointed.

At the end of the list I saw the name Shirley Gee. She lived in Inglewood and was nineteen years of age. I left that name for last because I thought she was too young. I finally called her but she had moved to Hollywood. Her grandmother told me she had moved and explained Shirley's circumstances. She was working in the Hollywood Presbyterian Hospital and lived on Edgemont Street. She didn't have a telephone in her apartment.

I said, "Lord, I am going to try this girl and if she is the one, just show me and I will understand."

I began to think how to approach Shirley without giving her a false impression because of my language barrier. To go to her apartment—oh, no! She didn't know me and I would scare her! I thought I'd better call the hospital, so I did, but they didn't give me a chance to talk to her. It was not allowed to talk directly to any nurse except in an emergency. I left a message and my telephone number, pushed the button of my electronic secretary on "absent," and went to work. In two hours I came back and saw the red light on, but there was no message.

I called the hospital again to contact Miss Gee, but didn't have any success. The receptionist told me it definitely was not allowed to talk directly to any of the nurses unless it is an emergency. Maybe my case was an emergency—I mean in a good sense! The next day, I decided to go to the hospital and approach Miss Gee personally. I didn't have a very nice suit; yet I felt I should put it on in order not to make her feel that somebody from the street had come and was not for her. No, this is wrong, I thought. I am going to visit her just as I am, with my working pants and sweater. If she likes me the way I am, fine! Something good is going to be accomplished, finally. If she doesn't like me, still fine! I'll say, "Thank you for giving me a chance to see you. Good-bye and may the Lord bless you."

So I prayed again and asked the Lord to show me through my heart if she was my sweetheart. I jumped into my car and went to the hospital. The only available parking space was in the emergency lot. I parked the car, locked it, and didn't pay too much attention to the people around except the guard, whom I greeted very politely.

I rushed into the hospital to meet the "emergency" requirements and began to look for the answer to my condition of emergency—Miss Gee. I asked a few nurses where I could locate the young lady. They looked at me, probably confused or sorry I was not looking for one of them or happy they were not the ones! Finally, one went and gave the message to Miss Gee. I was anxiously waiting in the hallway to see what she looked like and to find out if she was going to be the one; or would I have to see many more, or would I have to remain forever single and just serve the Lord alone, without a life-partner? It seemed to me it took a very long time until a nurse began to come toward me, the one whom I thought went to look for the lady of my search. But she couldn't be the same one because she was too sweet looking. I looked at her and thought, She is too beautiful to be one of the girls whom I met through the list of the hopeless cases. My heart jumped when she was close enough for me to see her attractive appearance.

"Hello," I said with an unusually gentle voice.

"Hello!" she answered.

"Are you Miss Gee?"

"Yes, I am," and she turned red. (This was a good sign.)

Oh, it is too good to be true! I thought. "I am Mr. Dimov," I introduced myself. "You may call me Jim!"

"May I help you, Mr. Dimov?"

"Oh, yes! I am very interested in seeing you. Would you give me a chance to talk to you?"

"Yes," she said, and turned red again, and tried to leave because she was in a hurry.

"Wait a minute, please. I'm very happy you said yes. This is wonderful, and I would like to see you in your church if this is okay with you."

"Yes, it is!" I heard her answer as she tried to leave again.

"Just a minute," I said. "Let us make our arrangements more clear."

"I must go," she said. "I'll call you," she added as she began to walk away.

I wanted to keep her next to me as long as possible, but didn't because she had a duty, probably with a very sick patient.

"Only a moment," I insisted. "If you call my business telephone, you will not be able to reach me because I will be working in the office of a mission. Would you like me to give you the telephone number?"

"Yes, I would!"

I took my business card and wrote as fast and clear as

possible the telephone number and gave it to her. She took it and said, "Thank you," and began to leave very fast.

"Miss Gee, excuse me. Would you like to tell me what time you are going to call me?"

"I'll call you at 5:00 P.M."

"Thank you. I'll hear from you tonight. Good-bye."

"Good-bye," I heard her sweet voice, and she began to move her presence to someone more needy than myself. I followed her smoothly moving figure with my eyes and sensed in my heart that she was the answer from the Lord.

When she disappeared around the corner of the hallway, I realized my heart was jumping in my chest as if it intended to go out of my mouth. I visualized her slender, medium-size figure, her beautiful complexion and rosy cheeks, her big, blue, expressive, and bashful eyes, her immaculate nurse's uniform that was below the knee, and her beautifully shaped legs. Only one quality of hers didn't appeal to me—she had short hair!

This is not a barrier, I thought. If she likes me and loves me, she will let her hair grow the length I want.

All of her physical qualities appealed to me immensely. Now, I thought, I must discover what her lovely vessel contains. Is she a girl who loves the Lord and puts God first? Is she a born-again Christian according to John 3:3: "Jesus answered and said unto him, Verily, verily [which means, Truly, truly], I say unto thee, Except a man be born again, he cannot see the kingdom of God."

I must find out Sunday. But why am I questioning myself? The Lord already answered by giving me a very strong desire for this young lady. According to Psalms 37:4, she is the answer for my wife! Here is what the Psalmist says: "Delight thyself also in the Lord; and he shall give thee the desires of thine heart."

I began to pray and said, "Lord, my supreme desire is to

be a missionary! There is no doubt in my heart and mind. And it looks like I am going to get married before I become a missionary. You could work it out the best way, pleasing Your holy will. Yet, my desire is to become a missionary first."

I went to work in the mission and was happily waiting for the call. Many people called. I didn't pay any attention. But when the telephone rang because she dialed, I sensed it and ran to the telephone. A girl asked me, "How do you know it is for you?"

"I sensed it. Let me get to the phone—hello, Shirley!"

"Hello, Jim!"

"How is the young lady doing?"

"Oh, fine, and you?"

"Fine, thank you. Am I going to see you Sunday?"

"Yes, at 7:00 P..M. in the Fountain Baptist Church."

"Praise the Lord. I'm very happy."

"I must go," she said.

"It was nice talking to you, Shirley. I'll see you at 7:00 P..M. Sunday night, okay?"

"Okay," she said.

"Thank you and be a good girl."

She said, "I will! Bye-bye!"

"Good-bye, Shirley."

On Sunday, when the time came I rushed out of my house, locked the door, and ran to my car. In about eight minutes, I was at the Fountain Avenue Baptist Church. The service of worshiping the Lord Jesus had just begun. A few times, I looked through the congregation but couldn't see the young lady. I concentrated on the preaching of the Gospel of Christ and enjoyed every bit of it. An elderly pastor, a "full-blooded" Christian, almost bald except for a bit of perfectly white hair, was preaching with a voice as strong as a man in his thirties.

After the service, many smiling faces full of the love of the

Lord came around me and asked me countless questions. I don't know if I answered correctly because my mind and eyes were occupied with searching for the young lady. Maybe my new friends thought something was wrong with me, and they were right! When a gentleman or a lady falls in love, something is wrong for sure. The young people were crowding around me and I was carefully trying not to block a clear view from my detecting eyes. Two young couples came my way and I decided to ask them if they knew Miss Shirley Gee. The answer was negative and I continued to pop out my eyes looking for the desirable young lady.

Then quite a few people left and I thought Miss Gee had broken her promise or purposely changed her mind and didn't want to give me a chance to prove to her that I was the one she would like the best—to prove to her that she was the right girl for me. My heart was jumping all over my chest, using all its energy and last movements as a bird in a cage. It was directing my eyes not to get discouraged in searching for the partner of my personal life on this earth.

Suddenly my heart jumped joyfully and it almost shocked me. Two eyes pierced my heart and I almost couldn't believe my eyes. I tried not to miss the beautiful sight of the gracefully moving young lady, coming closer and closer to me. Shirley was really here! I smiled at her, but didn't get a response. She was constantly watching me with her big, expressive eyes, trying to tell me something was wrong. I didn't realize right away why she was acting like that. Then, it was clear—she didn't like the fact that I was surrounded by young girls and some boys. In her eyes, I read, "You should be looking for me and shouldn't stay there surrounded by young girls."

Then I went to her, warmly shook her beautiful and gentle-as-velvet hand, smiled at her again, and got a friendly smile as a result of my warm greeting. Her beautiful pink cheeks turned red and it made me feel good. I took her by the arm and led her to my lovely white Buick sports wagon. She unbuttoned her gray coat and I saw her lovely figure, dressed in a beautiful, light green dress made with good taste.

I was very happy and decided to treat the young lady in the European Christian way. I opened the door of my car, took her gently but strongly by the arm, helped her to get into the car, and warmly welcomed her into my beautiful vehicle. When she had situated herself comfortably on the front seat, I closed the door and ran around the front of the car, jumped inside, sat behind the steering wheel, turned on the ignition, and began to drive to another church much bigger and more modern than the first.

Shirley liked the fact that I was driving her from one church to another. The service in the other church began much later and we were just about on time. There was a Russian choir singing beautiful Christian songs. Many Russian people were there from San Francisco and Los Angeles. The pastor of the Russian church from San Francisco was explaining how the Lord led a big group of people out of Russia in the most miraculous way. I took good care of Shirley, but she was not very comfortable. She was watching every move I made and every person who said hello to me. It looked like she was testing my situation as a single man. I introduced her to a few friends and thought it was too dangerous to do so because somebody could take the young lady away from me.

A few minutes after the service was over, I felt a strong desire to be alone with Shirley and in no time, led her to the car. We got into the vehicle, left the parking lot of the church, and drove slowly north on Brand Boulevard in Glendale. Shirley had fixed her hair very nicely and altogether, she looked lovely. She was not talkative, and I had to lead the conversation. That fact made me feel very happy and very important, and the bashfulness of the young lady attracted me strongly. I tried to make her feel as comfortable as possible, and to show her how much her presence meant to me and how important she was in my life.

"May I call you just Shirley, instead of Miss Gee?"

"Oh, yes, indeed," she answered.

"You can call me Jim, okay?"

"Okay."

"Listen to me very carefully. I am going to describe in miniature my humble Christian requirements. I'll be very honest with you, as I've been with all the girls I've been in contact with. I was raised in a Christian home, and my principle always has been: Before God and man, honesty always is the best policy. I've always put God first. How about you?"

"This has been the same principle for me. God is really put first in my life," she said.

"This is beautiful!" I encouraged her. "I have been looking for a long time to find the right girl friend, and all the doors were closed. Tonight I am going to tell you how little I require of the girl I want to marry. First of all, she must love the Lord with all her heart. I was raised in a very old-fashioned community and would like her not to be modern and worldly looking. As a Christian, I have a very simple formula about the girl I would marry. She must be a PPY girl."

"What does that mean?" Shirley asked.

"Naturally, you wouldn't know, because it is my own formula. Here is the meaning. PPY are the first letters of three words: Pure—Poor—Young."

"I am that kind of a girl," she said.

"Are you really?" I asked, amazed.

"Yes, I am pure because the Lord washed me in His blood. He protects me and more than that, I never have dated any boy. I am poor; this also is a fact, and I am young—only twenty years old."

"I thought you were nineteen years old."

"No, the information you got was given a year ago."

"Shirley, did you say you never had a boyfriend?"

"Yes, it is true, and I was just praying to the Lord to send me the right boyfriend, and here you are!"

I was so happy that if I didn't have to drive, I would have grabbed her, embraced her, and declared, "I have chosen you to be my wife!"

Shirley Marie was preserved by the Lord just for me. Many times, I described to my friends the kind of girl I was looking for. PPY—old-fashioned, bashful, and a good Christian who puts God first. This was a miracle! In the twentieth century and especially in California, to find a bashful girl is a miracle indeed.

"Shirley, I like you very much."

She turned red.

"You are a real treasure. I am very interested in you! Like every young, strong, and healthy man, I want to get married. Up to now, nobody has impressed me as much as you do. Let us pray and ask God to destroy every barrier if it is His will."

We didn't realize how the time went by, and I suggested taking her home. She agreed because it was almost 11:00 P.M. and she had to get up at 5:00 A.M. I drove her to the apartment, and I didn't want to leave her alone. My love for her was so highly developed, I was literally afraid to lose her.

"Well, Shirley, I would like to see you Tuesday. Is it all right with you?"

"Yes, Tuesday is all right with me."

My heart was jumping all over my chest and again, I was almost choking for joy. It seemed like she didn't want to leave me, also. I reached out my hand to shake hands, and she put her soft, gentle hand into mine. It seemed to me her hand melted in mine. It literally disappeared into my hand! A strong magnetism made me pull her hand to my lips and I kissed the soft and sweet skin of her hand. Then I pulled her to me and kissed her burning red cheek and almost fainted with joy. Her cheeks were red as a rose, soft as velvet, and sweet as a peach. I wanted to kiss the other cheek, too, but didn't. I thought I might scare the young lady.

I noticed that Shirley's eyes turned red and she almost cried for joy. I helped her get out of the car and took her to her apartment.

"I'll see you Tuesday, Shirley. God bless you! Good night and sleep well."

"Good night," she said, and I felt she didn't want to go inside.

I went home amazed that the Lord brought to me the best girl in the world—a girl who had never had a boyfriend— nothing was out of my formula. She was just what I was looking for—a PPY girl. That night, I couldn't eat or sleep. I liked quite a few girls, but I had never been in love like this time. All night long, I thought of her and hardly slept. I got up early in the morning and was very much awake and pre- pared to spend my energy in work. I had my personal morn- ing devotion, then tried to eat, but my appetite was gone. I jumped into my car and went to work. When I finished my job, I came back home early in the afternoon, not happy about the fact I had to wait two long days to see my sweet- heart.

No—I can't bear it, I thought. I am going tonight to see her and I don't care, even if I did say, "I'll see you Tuesday." I am sure she would understand and maybe she would like the idea. In no time I got ready and at about 5:00 P.M., I was climbing the stairs to the second floor, where the young lady lived.

Oh, no, I thought. It can't be true! A young man was stand- ing at the entrance of Shirley's apartment and talking to her. I almost jumped on him and thought I would "slay him down" on the balcony walkway. Shirley couldn't see me while I stood at the last step of the stairway. She had told me no boyfriend was involved! Just when I was not planning to see her, she was seeing this other man. My heart was beating very fast. He didn't look like a Christian to me and maybe this was an accident. I was controlling my desire to interrupt the conversation between Shirley and the young man. If I went between them at once, I could scare Shirley. No, I would wait. In a few minutes, the young man left and before Shirley could close the door, I jumped in front of her and said, "Shirley, good afternoon!"

I was brokenhearted. She jumped back into the apartment and gripped her heart.

"Jim, you scared me!"

"I am sorry! Who was this young man, Shirley?"

"A salesman! Why did you come today? Didn't you say you were coming tomorrow evening?"

"Yes, Shirley, but I couldn't bear waiting. Aren't you happy I came tonight?"

"Yes, but you should have let me know. I am not ready to go out tonight."

"That is all right, Shirley. I'll wait until you get ready. May I come in?"

"No, I would like you to wait outside."

I didn't like the fact that she didn't let me in.

"Nobody ever gets into my apartment," she stated, "and I will not let you in."

"Okay. I'll be waiting outside. Don't hurry; just take your time."

"I'll see you a little later," she said, and locked the door in front of me. In about fifteen minutes, she came out smiling, full of youth, life, and beauty. I took her by the hand and led her down the stairs. She pulled back a little bit and told me, "I don't want people to see us so close to each other."

Her bashfulness, purity, youth, and beauty were attracting

me more and more. In no time, Shirley became part of my
personal life. I was the happiest man in the world. I felt very
strongly that the Lord had planned our lives to melt into a
couple. I helped her get into my car and hurried in myself
and said, "Here we are again together, Shirley. Aren't you
happy we are together one day earlier?"

"Yes, I am happy."

"I presume you are hungry, aren't you?"

"No, I'm not."

"Neither am I. Shirley, I couldn't sleep last night."

"Neither could I," she said.

"Well, let us see where we could go. How about the Room
at the Top on Vine and Sunset?"

"What is it, Jim? Is it a restaurant or a place of amusement?"

"It is a restaurant at the top of a very tall building called
Federal Savings and Loan.

"Okay. Let's go."

We went and I felt very important when I helped her out
of the car. A parking attendant took care of the vehicle. We
took the elevator and arrived at the beautiful restaurant
called Room at the Top. A waiter seated us next to a window,
from where we could watch the traffic and the beauty of
Hollywood and part of Los Angeles. All the lights were sparkling like enormous diamonds and could capture the eyes
and take away the breath from anyone.

I ordered a salad and she ordered a small dinner. My appetite was literally gone! Nothing could disturb me while I
observed every movement of the young lady. Her beautiful
blue eyes seldom could be seen because she was looking
mostly down. I think bashful girls are the most attractive
ones. It gives the young man a chance to win them. If a girl
runs after a man, she devalues herself by showing her weak-
ness. Many men who want the ladies to run after them are

weak ones, because they do not have the strength to win their partners. In most cases, when the lady runs after the man and they get married, the marriage is not stable.

"Shirley, what do you think about rights between husband and wife? How much rights should each one have?"

"I think they should each have fifty percent," she said.

"Well, Shirley, that means you have fifty percent of the responsibilities of the home, which is quite a bit for a lady like you. Fifty percent of the burden regarding income and taking care of the home is yours."

"Oh, no. I changed my mind. Ninety percent to the husband and ten percent to the wife."

"My opinion is different, Shirley."

"Tell me, what is it?"

"I think the best couple in the world is one which puts God first. The husband has a hundred percent of responsibilities and rights as the head of the wife according to Ephesians, the fifth chapter. The wife has a hundred percent of responsibilities and rights regarding her position in the home. She should obey her husband in everything according to Ephesians, and her husband should love her as his own body. Shirley, do you agree with Ephesians, chapter five?

"Yes, I do."

"I would like to tell you a true story. One day I called a friend of mine. During our conversation she asked me, 'Jim, how are you going to treat your wife after you are married? Are you going to treat her as a slave?'

"'Why do you think so?' I asked her.

"'Well, I heard people in the old country like yours treat their wives as slaves!'

"'I am from the old country, but never heard that anybody treats his wife as a slave. When I get married, I'm not going to treat my wife as a slave or as a Bulgarian or as an American. I'll treat my wife as a Christian! When I get married, I'll elect my wife to be the queen of my home and she will be the happiest girl in the world!' "

"Shirley, you are invited to be the queen of my home. Are you willing to accept this exclusive invitation?"

"Well, I would like to pray, Jim."

"Oh, haven't you prayed yet?"

"Yes, I have, and I am praying now. Besides, I have to ask my parents, too."

"That is perfectly all right, and I admire you for that and I respect you more for the fact you are praying and also honoring your parents by asking them. Still, remember, you are not going to live with your parents, but with your husband. So when God does answer you in your heart, you have to make the final decision! So I'm going to expect the answer tomorrow. Talk to your parents and don't be discouraged in any case. Okay?"

"I'll try to do my best, Jim!"

"Shirley, you are the best girl I ever met! You dearly love the Lord and are a PPY girl. I believe with all my heart the Lord is going to join us to become the best couple on the earth! I never had a girl friend or a love affair. You never have dated, and this makes you very precious to me. I know it is not wrong to date the person you think is the right one. If I did not intend to marry a girl, I wouldn't date her either! My Christian understanding is, be honest because honesty before God, my Saviour, man, my fellow brother or sister or friends, is the best policy."

The time went by and we arrived in front of the building where Shirley's apartment was located.

"Well, Shirley, it is time to go home. Isn't it awful how time flies so fast!"

"Yes, it is," she said. It was getting close to midnight. I helped Shirley get out of the car and accompanied her to the apartment. Suddenly, I was thrilled to hear Shirley saying, "Jim, I cannot separate myself from you!"

"Oh, Shirley, it is very sweet of you to say so. I feel the same way. We have known each other only two nights, and I think and feel like I've known you for ages. Be a good girl and sleep well! Okay?"

"Okay, I will, Jim."

I kissed her gentle hand and her pink cheek, which was as sweet and soft as a paradise apple.

"Good night, Shirley."

"Good night, Jim."

"I'll see you tomorrow night, okay?"

"Okay, Bye-bye."

A strong desire to be together was attracting us so powerfully that we had to use all of our strength and willpower to separate from each other for the night. I went home excited about the future which God had ordered in our lives. For a long time, I prayed to God to direct us to the right decisions which were to be made in the near future. For a long time I couldn't sleep. I was involved in the function of my imagination, which brought me to all kinds of high places like hills, mountains, the moon, all the stars in the sky, and beyond the sky to heights only the faithful Christian could reach and see through the eyes of his simple faith in the Lord Jesus Christ.

Finally, I fell asleep and got up early in the morning, shaved, washed, and in no time, ran to make some extra money for my future life—the life of my marriage. The day went by very slowly. All my thoughts were concentrated on my missionary future and my married life. I went on time to see my little birdie, Shirley. She was all dressed up, and I noticed her beautiful eyes, which seldom were looking at me, were anxiously waiting to see "his majesty." When I came, her beautiful cheeks turned red, as always.

"Shirley, dear. Hi! Did you sleep well?"

"No!"

"Neither did I. Something has happened to me the last few days. I cannot sleep or eat!"

"I am in the same condition," she said.

"Shirley, did you talk to your parents, especially to your dad?" (I knew that her mother was her stepmother.)

"Yes, I did!"

"What did he say?"

"He told me it is up to me."

"Oh, this is the best answer a dad could give to his daughter. Now, let us see where we stand! I am literally sick about you. There is no girl in the world who could take your place in my life. Would you like to go to the Los Angeles Zoo?"

"Okay, let's go, Jim."

It was about 4:00 P.M. when we arrived at the zoo. In half an hour, the zoo was to be closed, so we decided to walk in the neighborhood of the zoo, which is full of hills, trees, and bushes.

"Shirley, dear! Would you like to come with me to the top of this hill?"

"Yes, Jim, I would, but I doubt if I'll be able to climb to the top because it is very steep!"

"I'll help you, dear. With the help of God and my help I can guarantee you we will reach the top of this hill!"

"Okay. Let's go."

I helped her get out of the car, grabbed her by the hand, and we ran, full of joy and happiness, to climb up to the top of the hill. I was praying to the Lord to give me strength to help Shirley and to get to that beautiful spot of nature created by God just for us. We began to climb together, but I had to place Shirley in front of me in order to protect her from falling and rolling down the hill.

A few minutes later, we were at the top of the hill, happy and victorious. We were smiling at each other, rejoicing in the presence of the Lord and in the presence of each other, satisfied with the success of our arrival. In a space of about twenty feet in diameter, there was only green grass. We were surrounded by trees. Alone with God ("For where two or three are gathered together in my name, there am I in the midst of them" [Matthew 18:20]), we continued to smile at each other and it seemed to me because of the beauty of nature and the beauty of the two young "doves," our breath was taken away.

During the sunset, the sunbeams were still finding their way between the branches of the trees and were beautifying our private and natural palace with golden ornaments, which were disappearing and appearing one after another. Soon it became very dark. Both of us were speechless for a while. It was very quiet, very private, very sweet. It looked like everything around us was engaged in beautifying our Christian love affair. God Himself took time to join us in the most beautiful wedding ever conducted by Him.

"Shirley, dear—I love you!"

She was silent and speechless. I thought, This is too beautiful to be true.

To Shirley I said, "Shirley, dear, can you hear me? I love you."

She continued to be speechless. It seemed as if she were in a trance. I wanted to wake her up, but couldn't. It was time to act manly! I grabbed her by the waist and picked her up off the ground.

"Shirley, dear, can you hear me? I love you!"

"Yes, I hear you!"

She didn't have the strength to respond, so I decided to help her!

"Shirley, dear, repeat after me; say, 'Jim, I love you!' "

"Jim, I love you."

"Oh, Shirley, you mean it, don't you?"

"Yes, I do."

"You are the sweetest girl in the world. Shirley, you are so beautiful! Will you marry me?"

"Yes, I will!"

"Oh, Shirley, am I dreaming? Are you sure you want to marry me?"

"Yes, I am sure."

"Well, this is a real victory. This evening we made the greatest decision—to join our lives."

I picked her up again in the air and our lips became joined together.

"Shirley, you are sweet indeed. Do you realize that soon you are going to be my wife, and I will be your husband?"

"Yes, Jim, I realize that."

"Shirley, I didn't realize how fast the time went by. We have to go to our homes in a short while. Remember, dear, that love is just like a beautiful red rose. It is very attractive, very desirable, but full of thorns. You and I must fight against all the thorns. We should never allow anything to disturb the purity and the beauty of our love.

"Remember, Shirley, dear, many could come around us to destroy what God has given us—to be united in a marriage which never existed before. The devil himself will try to do his best to destroy us by bad thoughts against each other or by using others, but the One who lives in us is much stronger than the one who is in the world. ('. . . greater is he that is in you, than he that is in the world' [1 John 4:4].) You and I, both of us, are joined to face the whole world and to fight, heart by heart, against the evil of this world in the name of our Lord and Saviour, Jesus Christ. Any fight against the evil one in the name of the Lord, our God, is a guaranteed victory! Isn't it?"

"Yes, Jim, I believe that with all my heart."

"I don't like to say good night but I have to because you are supposed to get up early in the morning," I said. "Good night, sweetheart, sleep well. I'll see you tomorrow."

"Good night, Jim. I don't have the power to separate myself from you."

"I'll help you, dear."

I led her by the hand, holding her by the waist, and we arrived in front of her apartment. I kissed her good night on her hand and both cheeks, and I left feeling strongly attracted to her, controlling myself, trying not to lose my balance going down the stairs. I was like a drunk, unbalanced because of the sweetness of my love for the young lady. Literally every night after that, I was dating her and our love was growing mightily stronger and stronger. It is impossible to be in love to this extent without faith in Christ, the only Lord. I don't care who you are. Actually, I do care; I love you in the Lord, Dear Reader; yet I must declare, if you have everything in this world which the carnal person could require and you do not have Christ in your heart, you have nothing! Your heart has nothing but the evil of this world—the devil himself. You may not realize this fact, but think for a moment. Check out your personal capacity, your heart. It is empty of the happiness of real love. Be honest with yourself. Give account to yourself. Isn't your life full of lonesomeness and misery? That's the condition of every non-Christian. I would be in the same miserable condition, but thank God, He opened my spiritual eyes through His Word, the Bible, and now I see far beyond the human imagination through the eyes of my faith in the Lord Jesus Christ, the Author and Finisher of my faith (*see* Hebrews 12:2).

The next night, like every night, I met Shirley, full of energy, joy, and happiness. I opened the subject of our wedding.

"Jim," said Shirley, "I don't want to have a wedding. Let's elope."

"Shirley, dear, I would love to elope. But we'll miss the blessing of the Lord and the people of the church, which is the body of Christ."

"Jim, how could I face so many people watching me? I'm

very bashful and I don't think I could bear the eyes of so many people watching me in the church."

"Shirley, dear, trust the Lord. He will give you courage and strength. I want you to concentrate your thoughts and heart on the Lord and on me. You will see how beautifully you are going to demonstrate your ability to be a lovely bride walking down the aisle of the church. Oh, how could we miss such a beautiful moment of our lives? After the wedding you and I are going to be so happy and thankful we didn't elope."

"Oh, Jim, that's true, but I really am not used to being in front of many people and I think we could elope and put an end to all the wedding-preparation troubles and expenses."

"Shirley, dear, I understand you, and would like you to understand me, too. If we do not have a wedding, we are going to miss the blessing the Lord has for us and the blessing of our friends in the church. In the future, God willing, we are going to have children who would love to see our wedding pictures. How nice it will be when we are visited by friends to have the wedding pictures to show to them. The wedding pictures will be a testimony of an example of a Christian wedding. Regarding expenses, I will pay all costs and you are going to be free of any financial obligation."

"Oh, no, Jim! Here in America, the bride pays all the expenses, and I have to work a few months to save money for the wedding."

"That is all right, Shirley. I am willing to wait."

So we settled down with a decision to have a wedding.

11

My Dreams Come True

One day a friend called and said she had talked to the pastor of a Lutheran church, who was very interested in hearing my testimony in his church. I was very happy and accepted the invitation. Everything was going so fast, so excitingly, so amazingly, that I purposely had failed to share my testimony with Shirley. I invited her to come with me, and she was very happy to be able to hear my testimony. At that time, Shirley had chosen the date of our wedding. I jumped when Shirley said, "Jim, I would like our wedding to be on the twenty-seventh of June, 1970."

"Wherever the Lord leads, dear," I told her.

"This date is very convenient and actually, it is the only date open for the wedding," she said.

"It is fine with me; praise the Lord. I am very happy and you are going to find out why!"

We prepared ourselves and went to the church. We were very warmly accepted among the Lutherans. I felt I was among real brothers and sisters in the Lord. We heard a few beautiful songs by the choir, which was conducted by the wife of the pastor, Mrs. Mathre. The pastor went to the pulpit, read some Scripture, spoke a little bit, and invited me to the platform. The Reverend Mathre introduced me very kindly to the audience and I took over the meeting.

I thanked the pastor for introducing me and for giving me this great privilege to glorify the name of the Lord in his church. I opened my Bible and read the fourth verse from the Twenty-Third Psalm. "Yea, though I walk through the valley of the shadow of death, I will fear no evil: for thou art with me; thy rod and thy staff they comfort me." I spoke for one hour and twenty minutes.

Nobody left the service. The audience was listening with great interest, especially Shirley, who was lost in my testimony. I realized she was very happy because she was amazed, like the rest, at how the Lord protected me from the dogs and the Communists, and how He answered my prayer by leading me and showing me it was His will for me to be in the West by the sign of number seven.

"Now, I would like to ask you a question. How many of you have seen an angel lately?"

Nobody raised a hand.

"How many of you understand my English?"

All of the listeners raised their hands.

"So there is no problem. Well, I would like to show to you what an angel looks like."

I asked Shirley to stand up. All the people turned to look at her. She blushed and smiled happily.

"This is my angel, Miss Shirley Gee, and she has chosen the twenty-seventh of June to be our wedding day. Before the service, she didn't know anything about my testimony, and she has chosen the right date, hasn't she? Praise the Lord!"

When the meeting was over, Shirley ran to me and asked me, "Jim, why didn't you tell me about your experiences with the Lord, and the answer to your prayer with number seven?"

"Well, dear, I wanted the Lord to lead you to the right date."

"Oh, this is amazing!" Shirley said.

Quite a few Christians asked me different questions, and all of them greeted me warmly and said how much they enjoyed my testimony. One Christian brother came to me, and I noticed tears were rolling down his cheeks.

"Brother Jim, I am astonished by the way the Lord led you over the border. My heart is moved and heavily burdened about our Christian brothers and sisters behind the Iron Curtain. Brother Jim, I want you to start a mission! And I want to assure you the Lord is going to bless you abundantly. I am a born-again Christian and I want to help you in the mission. I would like you, Brother Jim, to keep in touch with me. Here is my business card. Call anytime for money, and I mean it! I know it is very hard to start, but nothing is too hard for the Lord. Remember, with the Lord's help, I am going to back you up completely, because my heart deeply goes out to the Christians behind the Iron Curtain. We have some people who go to church for over twenty years, and they never accept the Lord into their hearts. I feel it is not right to overfeed some and to let others starve to death for lack of spiritual food. Besides, I am tired of giving and not being able to see the results of my contributions. Many American Christians are looking for the right mission to donate their gifts to because they are tired of being cheated."

"Brother, this has been the desire of my heart for eighteen years. You are the first man who has approached me in this most warm way and touched the most sensitive area of the supreme desire of my heart—to be a missionary. I am convinced, dear brother, that the Lord is using you to make my dream come true. I promise before the Lord, I am going to obey the voice of our Lord. This church is the beginning of a new ministry concerning feeding and satisfying the spiritual thirst and struggle of millions of born-again Christians behind the Iron Curtain. It is very sad when I see Christians who are cold and literally do not care about others less fortunate than themselves. I doubt their Christianity. Actually, there are three kinds of Christians. Some of them are like sponges; you have to squeeze them to get substance. Some are like peach stones; you have to crack them to get the nuts. Some are tenderhearted Christians who need only to hear about the need and respond immediately. Dear brother, I thank the Lord, you are a tenderhearted Christian!"

"Brother Jim, we take our freedom and abundance for granted. The way you described the lives of Christians behind the Iron Curtain makes my heart ache for them."

"I praise the Lord for your concern, brother. (The tears were still rolling down his cheeks.) May the Lord bless you abundantly."

All the Christians greeted us, and the most exciting comments about underground Christianity came to an end. Shirley and I went to the car and left Montebello. My heart was jumping in my chest, rejoicing because my greatest dream had come true.

I took care of Shirley by driving her home and went to my house. I went in and found out everything was the same. No, something is not the same, I thought. Probably I've done something, and I never paid attention. Am I awake or sleeping and dreaming? Not at all! The joy of the Lord is bubbling in my heart. I'm in the deep river of happiness caused by the fact that I have become a missionary! I knelt on the floor of my house and prayed for a long time, asking the Lord to give me wisdom and strength to operate the mission according to His perfect will. For a long time, I couldn't sleep, lying flat on my small bed. The ceiling of the bedroom was cracked and many pieces of loose wallpaper on the ceiling were hanging silently, the only witnesses to my rejoicing. I spent many hours praising the Lord, rejoicing, and thanking Him for making my dream come true. Late in the evening, worn out by my happiness and joy, I gave up and comfortably fell asleep.

The next day, I went to the bank and opened a new account in the name of the new mission; the Lord gave me a name which I treasure very deeply: Underground Christian

Missions. It is underground because it is not legal behind the Iron Curtain. What is legal there but the Communist party? It is Christian because it spreads the Good News of the Gospel of Christ. It is missions because it has many actions which bring help to the Christians in the world of darkness called communism.

I continued dating Shirley, who had moved to Inglewood to her grandparents' home to save money for the wedding. She really had a goal—to save for our wedding. I had to save for our honeymoon trip. Besides all the excitement about our marriage, I had to be excited about something I cannot compare with anything on the earth—to be a missionary for the eternal Kingdom of God.

All the funds over and above my bills were carefully invested on the mission's account. I ran into all kinds of projects. Some people may call them problems, but I praise the Lord because He turns them into projects. The first one was to find faithful men to be on the board. All my good friends were very busy with their own affairs. Some of them responded and exciting events took place. In a short while, we were incorporated. Our lawyer wanted four hundred dollars to prepare the documents. Of course, I didn't have that much money.

It would be nice if I could get help from a mission in Glendale, California, I thought. Not very long ago, I had gone to see the head of the mission there to ask if I could work for his mission. He was very nice to me. He embraced me and kissed me in a Christian way. I thought this was a real Christian brother. He invited me to sit down and, smiling, asked me what he could do to help me.

"I need work, and if you need a helper in the mission, I would like to work for you."

"Have you been in prison?" was the question.

"No, I haven't!"

"Well, come and work for me. I'll pay you two dollars an hour!"

I was very surprised by his businesslike manner, instead of receiving a Christian answer. Now for a different approach. I had heard he was very successful financially, so he could be the person to approach. I believed I would be encouraged and would receive financial help from him, for he was the head of that mission. I dressed up nicely in the same suit I wore when I took Shirley out, and went to see the head of the mission for the second time. He came to me all smiling, hugged me, and kissed me again.

"Brother, I need your help! With the Lord's help, I started a mission for the Christians behind the Iron Curtain."

"It is okay! Just like another grocery store! If the people do not like one, they go to another. The same is the case with different missions!"

"Brother, I need four hundred dollars to pay the lawyer who is preparing the documents of the new mission. I'm working and in two months, I'll pay the money back."

"No, I'll not help you," he said, with a very cold tone. "Remember, nobody is going to help you!"

One shock followed another. I came to get help which he could give, but I didn't get it. Instead, he tried to discourage me. It is hard to explain how a big man like him could refuse to help a new mission. That year, his report about donations to his mission was over $1 million. I left his home, broken-hearted by the nominal Christianity of this man.

I called my lawyer and asked him to wait for the money. He was not very willing, but he had to. My business was very slow, but my trust in the Lord was very active, as always. All the money I made over and above my bills had to go for mission purposes!

The time went by very rapidly and before I realized it, the wedding date was only one week away. At that time, I got work from a very nice Spanish-speaking lady. All week long, I worked very hard to paint a two-story frame house. It was very old and desperately needed painting. Many times, I had to repair some rotten boards or nail others that were falling apart. The owner, Mrs. Garcia, told me, "Jim, I realize you need the money for your honeymoon trip. Here is the money! I'm paying you in advance, and I trust you to come and finish the work."

I was moved by the attitude of Mrs. Garcia. What a difference between the head of that mission, who was not a born-again Christian, and Mrs. Garcia.

Saturday, the day of the wedding, I worked until noon, got the money, thanked Mrs. Garcia for being so kind, and drove home.

Two hours later, dressed in a brand-new black suit (which I intended to pay for later), I left my house very excited and very happy to experience the most unusual event in my personal life. It was a beautiful day, and I was driving my white car to Inglewood full of joy because of the wedding. I tried to imagine what my bride would look like, how the people would respond to the ceremony. My imagination went to the beauty of having my mother and all my loved ones at the wedding. But it was a pity! The coldness of the Iron Curtain had blocked the way for visitation of my loved ones. Some are able to visit because they are not involved in political activities, or like me, escape; yet, there was great happiness and joy to be privileged to live in such a free country, to be privileged to become a missionary and to have a wedding. Oh, it was too good to believe! At this moment, I was going to my own wedding! Oh, this was beautiful.

Many friends of mine were there. The photographer took a few pictures of the men involved in the wedding. I was asked many times if I was nervous.

"No, I'm just very excited and happy," I answered.

The bride, with all her bridesmaids, was hidden some-where. In a short while, everything was in order. Five, four, three, two, one minute to the beginning of the wedding ceremony. At once, we heard the Wedding March by Men-delssohn, which took the attention of the audience of about 150 people. I walked first, followed by the best man and the ushers. Then came the bridesmaids, and at last the bride appeared, led by her father. The guests got up and turned and looked back to see the bride. Millions of goose bumps ran all over my body. I couldn't believe my eyes. Shirley looked like an angel in a beautiful white dress which she had made. She was walking slowly and smoothly, led by her father. My heart was jumping so fast, I thought I would choke. I was superhappy and it felt like my heart was going to run out of my mouth. I never expected my darling to be so beautiful. All the faces were smiling and satisfied with the smooth, brilliant appearance of the angel of my heart. All the people approved of the elegance of the choice of my heart.

"Delight thyself also in the Lord; and he shall give thee the desires of thine heart" (Psalms 37:4).

This is a real dream! Look at the real people, Jim, I thought to myself.

Shirley was coming slowly and looked like she wasn't walk-ing but floating down the aisle, which caused the congrega-tion to turn and watch every movement of my angel as she came to me. Shirley's dad gave her away and I had to take over the situation. Being very close, I took her by the arm, and we walked together to the pulpit. The pastor asked us to take our vows, and we knelt before the Lord. The pastor asked all the people to pray and he led the prayer. Then he pronounced us "Mr. and Mrs. Dimov," and said to me, "You may salute the bride."

Shirley picked up her veil and I put it down. She picked it up again, and I put it down again. A lady laughed, and then some of the people laughed. I couldn't understand what the pastor meant by, "You may salute the bride."

Shirley told me I was supposed to kiss her in front of the people, and I did. We walked victoriously back down the aisle, smiling at the excited audience. The ladies especially were wide-eyed, trying not to miss any movement of the young couple. When we were out of the sanctuary, all of the guests followed us to the reception. I was surprised by the great cake and beautiful, huge, heart-shaped arch made by my wife. Everybody came to greet us.

All kinds of jokes and tricks took place. Some friends of mine expressed how they felt the anointing of the Lord upon us. Everything went smoothly and beautifully. We left the reception hall, and the group followed us.

My wife threw her bouquet and a girl friend of hers caught it. I threw the garter and her boyfriend caught that. Everybody began to say they were going to get married. In a short while, they broke up with each other. A little later, they found the right partners and both got married. Isn't it amazing how the Lord used our wedding to form two more couples?

When the wedding was over, we loaded our car with presents and went to my wife's parents' home. My sister-in-law and my wife opened all the packages. It was exciting to find out what everybody had in mind to bless the newlyweds with. We left our relatives and went to the International Airport Hotel, where we spent our first night together. What a blessing of the Lord to see a couple just formed, sharing each other in absolute purity—brought together by the Lord Himself to build their nest on the eternal rock which is Jesus Christ, the only Lord. Naturally, we desired a Christian foundation for our marriage.

Early in the morning, we went to San Francisco. This was the city my wife had chosen, because she had not been there before. We spent two days there, touring the city. Then we went to a forest close by the city and enjoyed each other in the sweetest way, sharing about the future of our life. On our way back to Los Angeles, we stopped to see Hearst Castle, the richest private home ever built. George Hearst spent over $1 million every year for over fifty years just for antiques from all over the world. The castle has one hundred bedrooms, a very big library, two (outdoor and indoor) swimming pools, and all kinds of furniture and articles. We couldn't see everything because we were tired. We spent the night in the Lemon Tree Motel, and on the next day, arrived at our "poor" home where we had to sleep on the floor because we had no furniture.

In a short while we adjusted to each other and began to live a normal Christian life. I began to pray to the Lord to bless the mission and my wife joined me. One day, a friend of mine asked me to quit working for myself because the Lord laid it on his heart to pay my bills.

I thought this was too much to accept, but he insisted and told me to go on speaking engagements for the Lord.

So I left and for six months, was traveling alone in northern California (and at times with my wife), sharing my testimony and the life of my brethren overseas in Communist countries. Nothing is more exciting and precious than to be able to get to people of all kinds of denominations. In the beginning, to get into a church through a pastor was just like going through very thick ice. Many of the pastors excused themselves because they were too loaded with missionaries. I wondered why these pastors were not happy to get as many missionaries as possible in their churches.

Once I talked to a pastor and told him, "It is amazing how some pastors are open immediately for missionaries and others are not open at all."

He hung up on me.

Some are very suspicious and want recommendation letters; some are interested only in big "stars." Being one of the little ones, I didn't have a big success. But God! God is so big, so good, so loving: if a pastor closes the door of his church to a mission like this, he is closing out a great blessing from the Lord. He is literally robbing the poor brother and sister who desperately need the touch of every Christian in the free world.

It is time for every born-again pastor and believer to realize how important he or she is to the Christian life of the less fortunate person. Some of the pastors do not require any recommendation letter or any big reputation. Of course, they must be careful whom they allow to visit their churches! I will never forget my visit to Los Gatos, California.

When I travel, I go to a grocery store and get my food. Very seldom do I go to a restaurant (for saving purposes). I was in line waiting to pay for my groceries. An elderly lady with perfectly white hair smiled at me in a very sweet way.

"You are a Christian, aren't you?" I asked her.

"Oh, yes, praise the Lord," she answered. "Are you from here?"

"No, I'm from Los Angeles."

"Oh, that is interesting. What are you doing here?"

I explained to her about my missionary activity. She was so happy to hear about U.C.M.

"My pastor would love to have you in our church!" she said. "Here is his telephone number. Would you call him?"

"I'll be more than happy. Thank you so much and the Lord bless you abundantly."

I paid my grocery bill, went to the closest telephone booth, and called the Reverend Donaldson. I told him how I got his telephone number and asked him if he would be interested in showing our film *A Trip to the Underground Church* to his congregation. He was not only interested but told me he

would love to have me in his church. Right away he set up
the date, and I went to Dayspring Chapel in Los Gatos.
Brother Donaldson had been a policeman, but the Lord
wanted him to become the pastor of a church. When I met
him, I felt this man of God was literally radiating the love of
Christ, the Lord.

"Brother Jim, I've never seen you before, or heard about
you. Before you show the movie or share your testimony, I
would like to tell you how I feel about your ministry: 'The
Spirit itself beareth witness with our spirit . . .' (Romans 8:16).
Your ministry is a true one and from now on, our church is
going to support your work for the Lord on a monthly basis."

I was listening to him and was amazed at his great response
to the Spirit of the Lord. I was thrilled to hear a spiritual giant
in the Lord expressing his love to our brothers and sisters in
the Communist world (he knew nothing about this mission).
Oh, how we need people like Brother Donaldson! I showed
the film in his church; then I was invited to share my personal
testimony. I received a number of invitations from the same
church, and I'm sorry to say I couldn't respond to all of them.
Fellowship with Christians melted in the love of the Lord is
the most precious communication a person could have.
Brother Donaldson and his church are really serving the
Lord in the most honest and loving way possible. Since I
visited their church, they have never failed to keep their
pledge, which has increased a few times.

For six months, I was traveling from one city to another
and reached many denominations. It's amazing that when
the Lord opens the door of a church, the pastor cannot close
it. Almost all denominations opened their doors to this ministry.

I found out during my traveling that many Christians and
non-Christians are extremely concerned about this great
country of America. Among the many questions I was asked

was one I consider very important: "Could you tell me if there is there any danger of America being taken over by the Communists?"

My answer is, "Yes, there is no doubt about it."

There are three reasons why this has not already taken place. The first one is that America is basically a Christian nation. The laws of the land have originated from the Bible and the Christian faith is still dominant.

The second reason is that most Americans are not only literate but well educated to the extent that they can evaluate the political and economic issues for themselves (if they will).

The third reason is that most people have a good standard of living and are not starving or desperate as many people of other nations are who have fallen for the Communist poison.

There is a danger now because the underground Communists in this great country have succeeded in creating all types of confusion and fear in the people's minds (or have exploited these negative factors), and no doubt feel that the time is growing closer when their poison will be accepted by the disillusioned and dissatisfied citizens who do not recognize their tactics and maneuvers. A very real need exists to find a way to arouse and alert the people to the dangers we are facing, and to let them know there is no way out of our national dilemma except through Jesus Christ. The American people must exert every effort to evangelize their own and also the Communist world. The Communists are winning because of their willingness to sacrifice everything to make Communist slaves of the whole world.

How much more should the Christians be willing to sacrifice in order to spread the Gospel of Christ, which brings eternal life and removes the doubts and despair from the minds and hearts of the people.

About the end of 1971, I came back to Los Angeles, worn

out because of long traveling, all broken down physically. I asked the Lord to keep me like that—humble.

There are three conditions which keep a Christian in the best contact with the Lord. The first is to be humble. The second is to be again humble, and the third is again, humble. So in a humble spirit, I said, "Lord, You know my needs. I accomplished my traveling this year. For the new year, I would like to get more work than I could handle."

In the mission and in my private business, I became so busy! Literally, I was working up to sixteen hours a day in the mission and in my business. My first business is to be a missionary! My second business is to be a "universal handyman". For all the success in the mission and in my business, I give credit to the Lord. He began to bless me so much! Oh, what a Lord; what a Saviour! In 1973, the Lord blessed me so much I was able to give over eleven thousand dollars to the mission. The more I give, the more I receive: ". . . It is more blessed to give than to receive" (Acts 20:35).

So if you want to be blessed, begin to give. A Christian lady from the city of Delano, California sent twenty dollars to U.C.M., and wrote a short note in which she asked, "Is this a true mission or a fraud?"

How strange! She was not sure, but still sent her support. I am sure the Lord made her act like that to prove to her that this ministry belongs to Him. I called her and tried to explain. She cut me off and said, "Brother Jim, I'm sorry I wrote like that. Please forgive me. Since I sent help to your ministry, the Lord has blessed me so much, it is hard to believe."

In a week, she sent twice as much. Patiently, I was waiting before the Lord for great miracles and blessings through this ministry.

The Lord is so wonderful! More and more people began to join U.C.M. and became partners in investing in the eternal Kingdom of God. My business grew bigger and bigger until

I couldn't handle it—just as I prayed! What a Lord! I could hire over three hundred people if I were dedicated to my business. How could I escape such a great blessing, working for free in U.C.M.?

Why for free? The Bible says, ". . . the labourer is worthy of his hire . . ." (Luke 10:7). Yes, but the Lord is blessing me through my business, so I do not need extra salary. If I stop working for this mission, I will be the most miserable person on the earth. Why do I feel this way? Because I came from behind the Iron Curtain and I know what it means not to have a Bible. A Russian brother worked eight months to buy a Bible. Another sold his cow, the only supply of milk for his family, in order to get a Bible. I will never forget the night a Christian brother in Bulgaria came to me and said, "Brother Jim, this sister in the Lord desperately needs money. She wants to sell her New Testament. Would you be interested in buying it?"

Would I! I had been dreaming for a long time of having the Word of God for myself. So I paid her a good price for an old, torn New Testament. Immediately, I felt very important! I became the proud possessor of a portion of the Bible! All Christians in Communist countries who receive a Bible feel the same way.

So, if I hadn't prayed for my brethren behind the Iron Curtain today, I would feel very miserable. Why? Because I am part of the universal body of Christ. Nobody can convince me that I could sleep well at night if I haven't prayed and done something for my suffering brethren. I wonder how you feel about them. The Lord has melted my heart with compassion and love for them, and I hope and pray He will melt your heart as well. Some of you already have a great love for these precious ones, and LOVE IS GIVING—self, time, and material substance. The Word tells us, ". . . It is more blessed to give than to receive" (Acts 20:35). Many people borrow money even to buy Christmas presents for their loved ones, to express how they feel toward those they dearly love. How much more should we express our love to the families of martyrs and to countless brothers and sisters living in bondage to ungodly atheists.

Once in Bulgaria, I was looking for something in the bottom drawer of an old dresser and was amazed to find a New Testament, worn and missing its covers and quite a few pages. Only God knows and I, too, know how happy I was to have an extra New Testament.

At that time, many school students were forced to work for free on cooperative farms. I had that worn New Testament in my pocket. Two village ladies were walking on a muddy street. I approached them very tactfully and told them about the Good News of the Gospel of Christ. They were suspicious of me in the beginning, but I felt their hearts were open and very hungry for the Word of God. Later on, they listened with great interest. They were in a hurry, and I walked as far as I could and in the end, I gave to one of them the worn New Testament. They were so happy to receive such a precious gift.

Many thousands of Christians behind the Iron Curtain are preaching to millions without the printed Word of God. What a joy to preach the Gospel and to give the Word of God to the ones who listen, for "faith cometh by hearing, and hearing by the word of God" (Romans 10:17).

In the meantime, my wife got involved and began to help me in my correspondence with the new partners in this ministry. In about eighteen months, we got an exciting message: our life was blessed by God with a fruit of our love. The Lord had decided for us to have a baby. All our friends predicted a boy, but it happened to be a very beautiful girl, who brought a lot of joy to our hearts.

U.C.M. is a mission with many activities behind the Iron

Curtain, completely dedicated in smuggling the Bible and spiritual literature to the Christians in the world of darkness. Nobody in this mission receives a salary from the donations sent to help provide spiritual food to the starving multitudes overseas. The Lord has opened other sources to supply the needs of the staff involved full-time in the Lord's work. We at this mission do not believe in dictatorship but in high respect and consideration of all involved in distributing the Gospel of Christ.

Whether or not you are directly involved in this mission, you are more than welcome to make comments and suggestions. Write to:

Underground Christian Missions
P. O. Box 1076
Hollywood, California 90028.

Ask any question or request my book for free. We will be more than happy to respond to your request. Whether you give or not, you are more than welcome to be on our mailing list. Remember, you are necessary to somebody behind the Iron Curtain. All gifts are tax deductible.

Remember, Dear Reader, whether you are a Christian or not, the Christians behind the Iron Curtain are praying for you daily. My question is, are you praying for them the same way? I would trust the Christians to pray because they are melted in the love of God through Christ the Lord.

A Christian lady in a Communist country was concerned about getting a complete Bible for her Christian friends. None of them had ever seen a complete Bible at all. So they contributed and collected money to pay for the trip of the Christian from behind the Iron Curtain. She bought the ticket and went from one to another of the Communist-controlled churches, but couldn't find one Bible. She traveled all across a Communist land, and all together traveled about six thousand miles in her search for a Bible.

She ended up in a Christian home somewhere, all worn out from traveling, where she settled to spend the night. At that time, the Lord led an underground smuggler to visit that very home. About midnight, the smuggler entered that home, amazed to see about twenty Christians, not sleepy at all and anxiously waiting to see the messenger of God. He spoke Russian fluently and greeted the believers in the name of the Lord from the Christians in the free world. They were so happy to know that there are Christians who really care for them.

The underground smuggler opened his beautiful Bible and read from the Gospel of Christ. Then he put the Bible under his arm and began to preach. Immediately, he noticed all the believers were not watching his face anymore. All the eyes were concentrated on the Bible under his arm. When he finished preaching, he opened his traveling bag and took from it an armful of brand-new, beautiful Bibles, and gave one to everybody. Somehow the lady who was searching for a complete Bible was missed because she was in the corner of the room. She went to the smuggler and with trembling voice, asked him, "Brother, do you have a Bible for my people?"

He couldn't understand what she meant. A Christian brother explained that this sister in the Lord had traveled over six thousand miles in search of a Bible. She meant the people in her country, who hadn't ever seen a complete Bible. They preached the Gospel of Christ from a portion of handwritten Scriptures. The heart of the underground smuggler was moved with compassion. He took ten Bibles and gave them to that precious Christian lady. When she took the Bibles, her eyes turned red and tears, like rivers, poured down her cheeks. She could not believe her eyes!

Now, these Bibles are in the hands of faithful believers and I can imagine active, dedicated Christians copying by hand and distributing the priceless Gospel of Christ, the Word of God, away behind the Iron Curtain.

Working as a handyman, I needed a piece of wood to repair a door. Naturally, I went to the trash in the corner of the yard. To my greatest surprise, I saw a complete Bible on top of the trash! My heart shrank and I almost cried.

Then I said, "Oh, Lord, we could find the Bible even on the trash in this country."

There are literally millions behind the Iron Curtain who pray for over fifteen years to get a Bible. Are you the owner of more than one Bible? If so, you are very wealthy! During my life behind the Iron Curtain, I always wondered why Bibles came mainly from the United States. When I came to America, I found out why. Up to 80 percent of every missionary dollar comes out of America. Only 20 percent comes from other places in the world. No wonder the Lord has blessed this country so abundantly. Close to 60 percent of all the goods on the earth belongs to the United States of America, which represents only 6 percent of the world's population. My explanation is this: America is so blessed because of the missionary-minded Christians of this country.

When my wife and I were traveling in northern California, we were reading the Bible together as always. At that time, we were reading the fifteenth chapter of Matthew. I was especially impressed by the twenty-seventh verse regarding the Christian life in the world. "And she said, Truth, Lord: yet the dogs eat of the crumbs which fall from their masters' table."

Whether you realize it or not, you who live in the free world are at the Master's table, especially the people in the United States, who are literally flooded with Bibles, spiritual literature, radio broadcasting of the Gospel of Christ, and spiritual television programs. It is not like that behind the Iron Curtain. If the Christians in the Communist countries could have only the very crumbs of your spiritual food, it would cause indescribable joy!

There is an Iron Curtain, but not an "iron ceiling." Behind the Iron Curtain, in all Communist-controlled countries, live millions of deprived, persecuted Christian brothers and sisters. These Christians refuse, often upon penalty of death, life imprisonment, and horrible torture, to abandon their faith in Jesus Christ as Lord and Saviour. They are willing to suffer persecution and punishment for His sake. They are counted privileged to have even a page of Scripture, which is to be shared with the brethren. The necessities of life are often denied to a man, woman, or a child because they are believers in Jesus Christ. There are no lukewarm Christians behind the Iron Curtain! To profess Christianity is to be totally dedicated to the Lord Jesus Christ, to the point of being willing to endure torture, even death.

Yet, the persecution doesn't stop Christianity; it literally spreads Christianity. In Russia alone, there are over 14 million born-again believers! I would say 90 percent of them worship underground. Because the church is severely persecuted, it grows very rapidly. Every born-again believer is just like a nail; the harder you hit the nail, the deeper it goes.

Once I spoke in Oceanside, California. After the meeting, a brother in his early forties approached me in the most tactful way and said, "Brother Jim, I am very concerned about you."

"Why? What's going on?" I asked.

"Remember, the Communists are watching you right here in this country," he said.

I smiled and told him, "Brother, I do appreciate your concern. Thank you very much, but I would like to let you know that I am watching the Communists, also; and besides, the

Lord is on my side! Whom shall I fear? If they kill me, they will make their hands more bloody, and I'll get to heaven."

We as Christians must not be scared under any circumstances, but should continue preaching the Gospel of Christ without any fear. "... perfect love casteth out fear ..." (1 John 4:18).

With the increase of the church, the need for Bibles is desperate and unimaginable. When one Christian brother received a Bible, he couldn't bear the joy. He began to read and read nonstop for about twenty-eight hours, pronouncing out loud the living words of the Word of God in his own mother language. The words which bring eternal life to the human soul! The Bible is not only to be read behind the Iron Curtain, it is to be kissed and embraced! Dear brother and sister in the Lord, remember that and you are the rich brother and the rich sister! You are very necessary to somebody behind the Iron Curtain!

Brother, sister—Do you have a Bible for my people? The Lord bless you and help you to pray for the underprivileged and persecuted Christians, as they are praying for you.

Some Christians advise us not to bother with the Christians behind the Iron Curtain because it is not allowed. Some want us to negotiate with the Communists and get permission to bring the Bible to the Christians there in their lands. Some say God will take care of them and we should not get involved in this dangerous task.

All these are tricks of the evil one. To ask a Communist government for permission to bring the Bible to the Christians there means to ask the devil for permission. God and the devil cannot coexist. The Communists, in some cases, would welcome the negotiation just in order to get the Bibles so they could destroy them.

An underground smuggler went to a Communist country. A Communist tourist leader, at a very convenient moment, asked the smuggler to bring him a Bible, if possible, because there was not a Bible in his whole family. The smuggler didn't have a Bible at that time, in that language. He promised to bring the Bible, and the Communist tourist leader emphasized, "Please do not forget, because we really want the Bible."

The following year, when the smuggler returned to that country, the same tourist leader happened to be leading his group. At another convenient moment, the leader whispered in the most secretive way, "Do you remember what you promised last year? I bet you forgot!"

"No, I didn't," said the smuggler, and gave five Bibles to the leader, one for each member of his family.

Tears poured down the cheeks of the Communist tourist leader. (There are many Communists who are interested in the Bible, but they are not real Communists in their hearts —they are forced to be. A person who is sending Bibles behind the Iron Curtain is not only benefiting Christians but non-Christians—even Communists.)

That tourist leader did not have words strong enough to express the thankfulness for the Bibles because that family had been dreaming for years of getting at least one copy, and now every member has a copy!

I left many thousands of Christians in my country, and I will never forget what it means not to have a Bible. We at U.C.M. believe that all Christians in the whole world are part of the universal body of Christ, and when one part of the body of Christ is suffering, the other parts must take action immediately.

Let us not allow any Bible to fall on the trash heap. Let us save every spiritual crumb, and oh, how precious it is to give to the ones who cannot do anything in return but to pray for you. Remember, you are blessed because of the faithful daily prayers of millions of precious souls who live in the world of darkness.

One day, when we get to heaven, all of us are going to give an account before the Lord for our life on the earth. I'm sure God is going to look first into our spiritual hands for fruits. He is going to give us the ability to see the results of our actions on this earth and to recognize the brethren we've helped. Oh, what a joy it will be to see ourselves fruitful, in the presence of our Saviour and Lord—God's only begotten Son, who redeemed us for eternal life!

"For I was an hungred, and ye gave me meat: I was thirsty, and ye gave me drink: I was a stranger, and ye took me in: Naked, and ye clothed me: I was sick, and ye visited me: I was in prison, and ye came unto me" (Matthew 25:35, 36).

"Remember them that are in bonds, as bound with them; and them which suffer adversity, as being yourselves also in the body" (Hebrews 13:3).

Readers are invited to write to:

BROTHER JIM
P.O. Box 1076
Hollywood, California 90028

Read by: —
Mattie Marie